Purdey's Guide to Weymouth

Unofficial Guide to Weymouth
2024

Angela Timms

PURDEY

We walked into Weymouth and have had a few days of walking around the shops gathering together information. Purdey can verify that Weymouth is definitely dog friendly. There is a sticker which appears in shop windows to let you know that the furry friends are welcome.

Dog Friendly Weymouth is a page on Facebook. They campaigned to get shop owners to allow dogs into their shops etc.

Purdey and I have found everyone to be very welcoming of having a dog in their establishment. There are a couple of exceptions where dogs are not allowed. We have marked dog friendly places with a

TELL THEM PURDEY SENT YOU!

Facebook: Purdey's Guide to Weymouth

Tell them Purdey sent you...

Copyright © 2024 Angela Timms

All rights reserved.

ISBN: 9798325813023

DEDICATION

For Nan and Grandad Timms who first bought caravans on Littlesea when it first started. Thank you for the holidays and for the happy memories.

In Loving Memory of Oscar who loved Weymouth, his walks and the warm welcome and biscuits he was given in certain shops.

We do not charge anyone to be included in this Guide. We wanted everyone to be able to be included so we have found as much information as possible on the internet to start this off. We then contacted each business or place to ask them to check their listing and to add anything to it.
We cannot be held responsible for any erroneous information published in this publication and no views here are the views of the author or publisher unless I have commented.
We write it as we find it.

Some were excluded because we had heard bad things, one because they didn't want any free advertising.

SPONSORSHIP

We are inviting businesses to sponsor the guide. To sponsor they are invited to buy copies and either hand them out to their employees, sell them or give them to their favourite shop so that that shop can sell them.

If you would like to sponsor this publication please email us at serenitywildhare@yahoo.com.

ACKNOWLEDGMENTS

Cover image taken by the late Francis Underwood
With thanks for permission from Weymouth Beach
Donkeys.

1 STARTING YOUR HOLIDAY

The alarm clock screams out it's morning crow but today is different. Today it is heralding a day which is yours to use, your freedom, your time away from the mundane. The open road or railway track is calling you.

The morning has dawned on your holiday. The bags are packed. Suntan lotion waits expectantly in the washbag, and it is time to put your things in the car and the weeks of anticipation are over.

Have you checked your oil and water as my grandfather always used to say...

Do you have your breakdown cover and all those things you need for a long journey.

If you have a dog, do you have water and a bowl and have you remembered the dog

Tell them Purdey sent you…

lead?

People pack in different ways. Some pack for weeks, gathering the things they want to take, laundering, packing and getting everything ready for the special day. Others rush around the day before, but one thing is certain. Cometh the day the cases are packed, and the journey begins.

The miles pass by one by one in a certain progression. Behind you the stresses of life, in front the wonder of your holiday.

If you have been to Weymouth before then you will know all the things that it offers. If you haven't then this is your chance to experience something new.

Whichever, Purdey and I wish you a wonderful holiday.

> We hope that this guide will help you to find the interesting and worthwhile places in and around Weymouth.

PLACES TO VISIT

www.dayoutwiththekids.co.uk/things-to-do/south-west/dorset/weymouth

THE TANK MUSEUM
Bovington
www.tankmuseum.org   01929 405096
www.facebook.com/tankmuseum
visit@tankmuseum.org

BH20 6JG

The Tank Museum (once known as the Bovington Tank Museum) is a collection of armoured fighting vehicles at Bovington Camp. It is about 1 mile (1.6 km) north of the village of Wool and 12 miles (19 km) west of the major port of Poole.

The collection traces the history of the tank. With almost 300 vehicles in the exhibition from

Tell them Purdey sent you...

26 countries it is the largest collection of tanks and the third largest collection of armoured vehicles in the world. It includes Tiger 131, the only working example of a German Tiger I tank, and a British First World War Mark I, the world's oldest surviving combat tank. It is the museum of the Royal Tank Regiment and the Royal Armoured Corps and is a registered charity.

It brings the story of tanks and crews to life and you can see the tanks in action. It is family friendly.

They estimate a 4-5 hour visiting time and there is an onsite restaurant if you get hungry.

Assistance dogs are welcome but not emotional support dogs. It is not dog friendly due to the noise.

I remember many a happy day there climbing on the tanks. Not sure if you are still allowed but I'm sure there is plenty still to do.

Monday – Sunday   10:00 - 17:00

I remember visiting the Tank Museum many times over the years. It is always a fun day out. They used to let people climb on the tanks, I don't know if they do now but the things to do have expanded greatly. Looking at what is on offer there is much more on the educational and interactive side.

Tell them Purdey sent you…

ABBOTSBURY SUBTROPICAL GARDENS

www.abbotsburygardens.co.uk 01305 871387
www.facebook.com/AbbotsburySubtropicalGardens/
DT3 4LA

Travel the world in 30 acres. Jurassic Coast View, Burma Rope Bridge, Ponds and Wildlife, Specialist Plant Centre, Tea House, Quality Gift Shop.

The garden is Grade I listed in the National Register of Historic Parks and Gardens.

The garden was created in 1765. In the late eighteenth century, the Fox-Strangeways family (the Earls of Ilchester) built a new house on the location. This was burnt down in 1913, so they returned to their family seat at Melbury House, but the walled garden was maintained and remains in the ownership of the family. Since

Tell them Purdey sent you...

then, particularly after the contributions of the 4th Earl of Ilchester, the gardens have developed. It is now an 8 hectares (20 acres) site including exotic plants, many of which were newly discovered species when they were first introduced. There are formal and informal gardens, woodland walks, and walled gardens. The gardens also contain certain "zones" that exhibit plants from different geographical areas.

The gardens are in a wooded and sheltered valley, leading down towards the sea at Chesil Beach; this combination produces a microclimate in which more delicate plants than are usually grown in southern England can flourish, and plants that would otherwise need a greenhouse can be grown outside. However, in spite of its location, the plants remain vulnerable to bad winters, and the frost that they can bring. In 1990, violent storms damaged many of the rare specimens which have since been replaced by younger plants. In 2010, Abbotsbury employed the chainsaw artist Matthew Crabb to carve a 200-year-old oak tree that had fallen after a particularly bad winter.

The gardens won the Historic Houses Association/Christie's Garden of the Year award for 2012, the first time that a subtropical garden has gained the award.

Last entry to the gardens is 4pm daily
Adult   £12.95

Tell them Purdey sent you…

Disabled Adult + 1 Carer   £12.95
Monday - Sunday   10:00 - 16:00

ABBOTSBURY SWANNERY

www.abbotsburyswannery.co.uk   01305 871858
www.facebook.com/AbbotsburySwannery/
DT3 4JG

PLEASE NOTE: DOGS ARE NOT ALLOWED *for obvious reasons. There are swans about! We would not want the swans to be disturbed and it is not the ideal place for a dog.*

Willow swan maze, Giant Swan Nest & Outdoor Classroom, Audio Visual Show, Pedal Go Karts, Café and Children's Outdoor Play Area, Wild Flower Nature Meadow (May – Sept), Quality Gift Shop. Open 7 days. 10am – 5pm (4pm winter). Please check. Mass feeding 12 noon & 4pm.

Abbotsbury Swannery is a colony of nesting mute swans. Located on an 1-hectare (2-acre) site around the Fleet Lagoon protected from the weather of Lyme Bay by Chesil Beach, it is the only managed swannery in the world. It can be the home to over 600 swans with around 150 pairs.

Written records of the swannery's existence go back to 1393, though it probably existed well

Tell them Purdey sent you…

before that and is believed to have been set up by Benedictine monks in the eleventh century.

Monday – Sunday   10:00 - 17:00

GOLDEN CAP

www.nationaltrust.org.uk/visit/dorset/golden-cap
https://en.wikipedia.org/wiki/Golden_Cap

Golden Cap is a hill and cliff between Bridport and Charmouth. At 191 metres (627 ft), it is arguably the highest point near the south coast of Great Britain (although the highest point is set back some 250 m (820 ft) from the coastline) and is visible for tens of miles along the coastline. It is accessible via a coastal footpath from Seatown. It takes around 40 minutes to reach the summit.

The hill is owned by the National Trust and is part of the Jurassic Coast, a World Heritage Site.

The base of the cliff is covered with large boulders, and is popular with fossil collectors. Storms have previously exposed fossilised ammonites and belemnites in the Blue Lias base.

The name comes from the distinctive outcropping of golden greensand rock present at the very top of the cliff.

Behind the cliff you will find Langdon Wood, a small wood of mainly Corsican Pine, planted

Tell them Purdey sent you…

in the 1950s, whose trees originate from a nearby copse known as "Eleanor's Clump". Langdon is owned by the National Trust, and provides a circular walk of approximately one mile.

On a clear day you would be able to see Portland Bill, Start Point and Dartmoor in Devon

CORFE CASTLE

www.nationaltrust.org.uk/visit/dorset/corfe-castle
https://en.wikipedia.org/wiki/Corfe_Castle

Corfe Castle is a fortification above the village of Corfe on the Isle of Purbeck peninsula.

It was built by William the Conqueror in the 11th century.

It commands a gap in the Purbeck Hills on the route between Wareham and Swanage.

The first castle was one of the earliest in England to be built at least partly using stone when the majority were built with earth and timber.

Corfe Castle underwent major structural changes in the 12th and 13th centuries.

In 1572, Corfe Castle left the Crown's control when Elizabeth I sold it to Sir Christopher Hatton.

Tell them Purdey sent you...

Sir John Bankes bought the castle in 1635 and was the owner during the English Civil War. While Bankes was fighting in London and Oxford, his wife, Lady Mary Bankes, led the defence of the castle when it was twice besieged by Parliamentarian forces. The first siege, in 1643, was unsuccessful, but by 1645 Corfe was one of the last remaining royalist strongholds in southern England and fell to a siege ending in an assault when Lady Banks was betrayed by one of her garrisons who allowed Parliamentary soldiers to gain possession of the building. They then destroyed the edifice.

They toppled its mighty walls and undermined its foundations until nothing but the hollow shell that you see today remains.

Wraiths In The Ruins

An aura of mystery soon descended over the bare ribs of the once regal pile.

Strange, flickering lights were seen moving about the ramparts at night.

The heart-rending sobs of a weeping child were heard in a cottage that abuts the rocky knoll on which the castle stands.

A headless white lady, a shimmering shade who chills the blood of those who see her, and they find themselves shivering and shaking until she turns and drifts slowly away, fading into nothingness.

Free entry for National Trust members and

Tell them Purdey sent you…

under 5's.

Child ticket applies for 5-17 year olds (inclusive).

Family ticket admits two adults plus up to three children.

Family (1 adult) ticket admits one adult plus up to three children.

Carers: Disabled visitors and members can bring their carers / essential companions into our places for free.

2024 Peak

Ticket type	Gift aid	Standard
Adult	£14.30	£13.00
Child	£7.20	£6.50
Family	£35.80	£32.50
Family (1 adult)	£21.50	£19.50
Group Adult		£12.35
Group Child		£6.18

Monday – Sunday   10am – 5pm

PORTLAND CASTLE

Liberty Road, Castletown DT5 1AZ

0370 333 1181

www.english-heritage.org.uk/visit/places/portland-castle/

Portland Castle is an artillery fort which was constructed by Henry VIII between 1539 and 1541. It was part of the King's Device programme to protect against invasion from France and the Holy Roman Empire and defended the Portland Roads anchorage.

The fan-shaped castle was built from

Tell them Purdey sent you...

Portland stone and included a curved central tower and a gun battery, flanked by two angular wings.

It was armed with eleven artillery pieces, intended for use against enemy shipping, operating in partnership with its sister castle of Sandsfoot on the other side of the anchorage.

During the English Civil War, Portland was taken by the Royalist supporters of King Charles I, and then survived two sieges before finally surrendering to Parliament in 1646.

Portland continued in use as a fort until the end of the Napoleonic Wars in 1815, when it was converted into a private house. Fresh concerns over invasion led to the War Office taking it over once again in 1869, but the castle was not rearmed and was instead used as accommodation for more modern neighbouring fortifications.

During the First and Second World Wars it was used as offices, accommodation and as an ordnance store.

In 1949, the War Office relinquished control, and in 1955 it was opened to the public by the state.

It is managed by English Heritage, receiving 22,207 visitors in 2010. Historic England consider the castle to form "one of the best preserved and best-known examples" of King Henry's forts.

Tell them Purdey sent you...

Today it provides a great day out for visitors and its audio tour, included in the admission price, tells of the castle's 450-year history and the part it played in the First and Second World Wars. Portland Castle offers lots to do for families and couples alike, and only four miles from Weymouth, this historic adventure can easily be combined with some more contemporary seaside fun.

Enjoy stunning sea views from the gun platforms and get close to the powerful cannons. Then take a stroll in the Contemporary Heritage Garden.

- The free audio tour bringing history to life, from the Tudors to the Second World War
- The stunning sea views from the gun platform
- Exploring the 'herb garden' with our discovery pack
- A visit to the Tudor kitchen, armoury and gun platforms

You don't need to book your ticket in advance, but you will always get the best price and guaranteed entry by booking online ahead of your visit. If you are a member and wish to book, your ticket is still free. Your booking is for the site/event only and does not guarantee a car parking space, which may carry an additional

Tell them Purdey sent you…

charge.
Adult	£9.50
Concessions	£8.50
Children	£5.50
Family	£24.50

(2 adults up to three children) + donation,
Family   £15.50
(1 adult, up to three children) + donation.
Under fives free.

Monday - Sunday   10:00 - 17:00

PORTLAND MUSEUM

217 Wakeham, Portland   DT5 1HS
                                   01305 821804

https://portlandmuseum.co.uk/
www.facebook.com/PortlandMuseum/
portlandmuseum@gmail.com

Dinosaurs, fossils, shipwrecks and smugglers, stone carving, seafaring, groundbreaking scientists and world-famous authors: Portland Museum packs in an astonishing collection that reflects the history and people of this distinctive island community.

Staffed by volunteers from the local community, Portland Museum looks forward to welcoming visitors eager to find out about author Thomas Hardy and museum founder Dr Marie Stopes' connections to the island. Ancient superstitions in witchcraft, getting up

Tell them Purdey sent you…

close and personal with a Jurassic sea monster or finding out about the Nanny Diamonds, Portland Museum has something to interest everyone.

Adults	£5.00
Concession	£4.50
Child	£1.00
Family ticket	£10.00
Islanders and Friends of Portland Museum	FREE

Group rates by arrangement.

Saturdays – Wednesday   10:30 – 4.00
(last admittance 3:30pm)

RUFUS CASTLE

Church Ope Road, Portland   DT5 1JA
https://en.wikipedia.org/wiki/Rufus_Castle

There is no public access to the castle as it is privately owned, though it can be seen well from public footpaths along the coast.

In ancient times to pay for defence against attack, taxes were raised on the island to construct Portland's first castle. Rufus Castle was reportedly built for William II, although the structure seen standing in ruins today is not of that date. In 1142, Robert, Earl of Gloucester captured the castle from King Stephen on behalf of Empress Maud. It had additional fortifications added in 1238 by Richard de Clare

Tell them Purdey sent you...

who owned it at that time. Around 1256, Aylmer de Lusignan obtained a licence to crenulate the 'insulam de Portand' and Robert, Earl of Gloucester, was granted a similar licence just 14 months later. It is generally presumed that Rufus castle is the site of any work that may have resulted from these licences and any remains that may date from the period exist only at foundation level or have been lost to cliff erosion.

The castle was rebuilt between 1432 and 1460, by Richard, Duke of York, and much of what remains today dates from this time. The politician and writer John Penn built the adjacent Pennsylvania Castle, a Gothic Revival mansion overlooking Church Ope Cove, between 1797 and 1800. Penn's new estate encompassed both Rufus Castle and that of the former parish church of St Andrews. At this time Penn made alterations to Rufus Castle to transform it into a picturesque folly. He erected a bridge over the lane leading to Church Ope and formed two new large openings in the walls of the castle, with a rounded arch to the North Elevation and Tudor pointed arch to the South which replaced the original door to the structure. In 1989, the castle's seaward arch collapsed. By the end of the century English Heritage had proposed a restoration to preserve the castle.

Tell them Purdey sent you…

ATHELHAMPTON HOUSE

Athelhampton Road, Dorchester DT2 7LG

01305 848363

www.athelhampton.com/

Athelhampton is one of England's finest Tudor Manors.

The Great Hall built in 1485 remains greatly unchanged with a mainly original hammer-beam roof, carved stonework, stained glass, and other details. The house survives due to its complex ownership through the years.

Ghosts:
The Martyn Ape
The Grey Lady
The Hooded Priest
A Poltergeist - Professional assistance was used to allow this mischievous spirit to move on and there has not been a repetition since.
The Dualists
The Cooper
The Soldier
"Hello" - A recent newcomer to Athelhampton, a lady who says "hello".
The Bride
Most Haunted - This great ghost hunting TV show, hosted its first sleepover at

Tell them Purdey sent you…

Athelhampton with Yvette Fielding and Derek Acorah, this was a spine chilling episode.

www.athelhampton.com/onlineticket

Gardens:
Adult	£14.50
Student	£11.50
Child	£6.00
Infant	Free
Dog	£1.00
HH Members	Free
Carer	Free

House & Gardens:
Adult	£19.50
Student	£16.50
Child	£10.00
Infant	Free
Group	£12.00
HH Members	Free
Carer	Free
Restaurant & Shop	10am to 5pm
Gardens	10am to 5pm
House	11am to 5pm

last admissions to the House at 4pm

MONKEY WORLD

Longthorns, Wareham   BH20 6HH
                               01929 462537

www.monkeyworld.org/

Tell them Purdey sent you…

www.facebook.com/MonkeyWorldApeRescue

Ape Rescue Centre. Over 250 rescued apes and monkeys of 25 different species. Daily keeper talks, Largest adventure playground in the south, Café & Catering Kiosks, Picnic Areas, Gift Shop, Self-guided Audio Tours, Pre-booked Guided Tours, Children's Activity Centre, Accessible for all

Ticket prices: On Site/On line

Family (2 adults + 2 children/seniors)	£52.25/£48.00
Single Parent Family (1 adult + 2 children/seniors)	£38.00/£34.50
Adult	£19.00/£17.00
Student (NUS Student Card required)	£14.75/£13.50.
Child (3-15 years old)	£12.75/£11.50
Child (under 3 years old)	FREE
Senior (65+ years)	£12.75/£11.50
Disabled Visitor without Carer	£12.75/£11.50
Disabled Adult + 1 x Essential Carer	£19.00/£17.00
Disabled Child with 1 x Essential Carer	£12.75/£11.50
Disabled Senior with 1 x Essential Carer	£12.75/£11.50
Blue Peter Badge Holder (with badge & badge ID & accompanied by full paying adult/ senior)	FREE
Monday – Friday	09:00 - 17:00
Saturday	CLOSED
Sunday	CLOSED

Tell them Purdey sent you…

PORTLAND VIEW ANIMAL SANCTUARY

Osmington, Weymouth
www.facebook.com/profile.php?id=100092251785799
Portlandview.animals@gmail.com

Portland View Animal Sanctuary, based in Osmington, is safe space for rescued animals & wildlife.

Please contact them if you would like to visit.

We don't charge for sessions but do ask for a donation if possible. You can also adopt a sheep.

FUN DAY   STALLS AT EVENTS

Tell them Purdey sent you…

They do it because they care. Looking after farm animals is never easy. There are high points and there are low. The animals that come to them often need specialist care and that can mean a hefty vet's bill.

They love their animals and they love to introduce them to you. Also if you see them with a stall at an event why not buy generously. They deserve your help!

WEYMOUTH HARBOUR

01305 838423

https://en.wikipedia.org/wiki/Weymouth_Harbour,_Dorset
Webcam:
www.weymouth-harbour.co.uk/webcam/

Tell them Purdey sent you...

The harbour is the mouth of the River Wey as it enters the English Channel. The original Roman port at Radipole to the north was lost to silting (forming Radipole Lake), and the current harbour further downstream, lying between Weymouth Old Town and Melcombe Regis, started to develop in the 12th and 13th centuries. Weymouth Harbour opens into the much larger Portland Harbour to the south and east.

Weymouth Harbour has included cross-channel ferries but is now home to pleasure boats and private yachts. The Weymouth Harbour Tramway ran along the north side of

Tell them Purdey sent you…

the harbour to the long disused Weymouth Quay railway station. The track was removed during 2020 and 2021 except for two short sections left as a memorial. Immediately to the north at the harbour entrance is Weymouth Pier, separating the harbour from Weymouth Beach and Weymouth Bay. Stone Pier is located on the south side of the harbour entrance.

The harbour includes a lifting bridge to allow boats into the inner harbour, Weymouth Marina.

Bridge Opening Times

MAY	JUNE	JULY	AUG	SEPT	(1ST-15TH)
0800	0800	0800	0800	0800	0800
1000	1000	1000	1000	1000	1000
1200	1200	1200	1200	1200	1200
1400	1400	1400	1400	1400	1400
1600	1600	1600	1600	1600	1600
1800	1800	1800	1800	1800	1800
2000	2000	2000	2000	2000	2000
		2100	2100	2100	

Watching the bridge open can be highly amusing. There are set times and plenty of cafes and outdoor seating to sit, watch the boats go by and enjoy yourself. If you are on holiday, your time is your own. So enjoy it!

Tell them Purdey sent you…

WEYMOUTH BEACH

Webcam
www.camsecure.co.uk/weymouth_esplanade_webcam.html

The beach is a popular destination for beachgoing and was frequented by King George III for sea bathing during times of illness. The king named Weymouth his 'first resort' and made bathing fashionable there. George III was advised to take the waters after his first bout of porphyria.

Weymouth Beach is very wide and gently sloping, with golden sand and shallow waters normally with small waves. In addition to bathing, the expansive beach is used for beach motocross and volleyball.

The beach has the traditional attractions of an English seaside resort, including (during the summer season) donkey rides, Punch and Judy, sand sculptures, trampolines, a small funfair for children, and pedalo hire.

At the southern end is Weymouth Pier, including the Pavilion Theatre and Weymouth Sea Life Tower. At the northeastern end is the suburb of Greenhill, with Furzy Cliff and Bowleaze Cove beyond that.

The beach was voted Number 1 in The Times and Sunday Times Best UK Beaches 2023.

Dogs are permitted on the beach at the Pavilion end.

Purdey loves the beach. In the winter months there is access to the whole beach but in the summer just the bit near the pavilion. It still allows you to enjoy a day at the beach with your dog.

Tell them Purdey sent you…

The sand on Weymouth Beach is ideal for building sand castles. There are plenty of places selling buckets and spades but you can also get creative yourself.

SAND SCULPTURE
www.facebook.com/sandworldweymouth

There is also a building adjacent to the Esplanade on the beach where there is a sand sculpture either being completed or completed. You will be able to see the sculptor at work.

Weymouth sand is very suitable for sand sculpture due to the size of the grains and their shape.

Tell them Purdey sent you…

DONKEYS ON THE BEACH

07968 206745

westhilldonkeys@live.co.uk
www.weymouthdonkeys.co.uk/
www.facebook.com/beachdonkeys/

Image taken by the late Francis Underwood

All things donkey, rides on Weymouth Beach, fetes and parties. Donkeys for therapy visits. Appearances, parades, celebrations and so much more.

	£5.50/ride
Monday	CLOSED
Tuesday	11:00 - 16:20
Wednesday	09:00 - 17:00
Thursday	09:00 - 17:00

Tell them Purdey sent you…

Friday   09:00 - 17:00
Saturday   09:00 - 17:00
Sunday   09:00 - 17:00

Weymouth Punch & Judy Show

07974 732352
www.weymouthpunch.co.uk

www.facebook.com/weymouthpunchjudy/

Weymouth Punch and Judy is one of very last seaside shows left in the world. Please support it.

DURDLE DOOR

The coastline around Durdle Door is shaped by its geology. This is due to the contrasting hardnesses of the rocks, and by the local patterns of faults and folds. The arch has formed on a concordant coastline where bands of rock run parallel to the shoreline. The rock strata are almost vertical, and the bands of rock are quite narrow. Originally a band of resistant Portland limestone ran along the shore.

Behind this is a 120-metre (390 ft) band of weaker, easily eroded rocks, and behind this is a stronger and much thicker band of chalk, which forms the Purbeck Hills. These steeply dipping rocks are part of the Lulworth crumple, itself part of the broader Purbeck Monocline, produced by the building of the Alps during the mid-Cenozoic.

Around this part of the coast, nearly all of the limestone has been removed by sea erosion, whilst the remainder forms the small headland which includes the arch. Erosion at the western end of the limestone band has resulted in the arch formation. UNESCO teams monitor the condition of both the arch and adjacent beach.

The 120-metre (390 ft) isthmus that joins the limestone to the chalk is made of a 50-metre (160 ft) band of Portland limestone, a narrow and compressed band of Cretaceous Wealden clays and sands, and then narrow bands of greensand and sandstone.

As the coastline in this area is generally an eroding landscape, the cliffs are subject to occasional rockfalls and landslides; a particularly large slide occurred just to the east of Durdle Door in April 2013, destroying a part of the South West Coast Path.

Tell them Purdey sent you…

Lulworth Cove to Durdle Door Walk
www.dorsettravelguide.com/lulworth-cove-to-durdle-door-walk/

The Dorset Coast Path runs along that part of the coast. There are steps cut in and the path has been managed so it is reasonably easy to walk.

LULWORTH CASTLE & COVE

01929 400352

Main Road, WEST LULWORTH, BH20 5RQ

The cove is one of the world's finest examples of such a landform and is a World Heritage Site and tourist location with approximately 500,000 visitors every year, of whom about 30 per cent visit in July and August. It is close to the rock arch of Durdle Door and other Jurassic Coast sites.

PARKING

Pay on arrival. Lulworth Cove is open 24 hours.

The overflow field is locked at 9pm

All Day Parking (until 9pm or dusk)	£12.00
Up to 4 hours	£6.00
Oversize vehicles (Above 5.5m and up to 16 seats)	£20.00
Motorcycles	£2.00

Tell them Purdey sent you…

Coaches must pay
using the JustPark App   £30.00

Card payments only, or use the JustPark App.
   Tickets purchased at Lulworth Cove are valid at Durdle Door Standard, Newlands Meadow and Lulworth Castle.
www.justpark.com/uk/parking/lulworth-cove

PORTLAND BILL LIGHTHOUSE

Portland Bill Road, Portland DT5 2JT   01305 821050
www.trinityhouse.co.uk/lighthouse-visitor-centres/portland-bill-lighthouse-visitor-centre
   Portland Bill is a narrow promontory (or bill) at the southern end of the Isle of Portland.
   Portland's coast has been notorious for the number of shipwrecked vessels over the centuries. The dangerous coastline features shallow reefs and the Shambles sandbank, made more hazardous due to the strong Portland tidal race.
   The Bill is an important waypoint for coastal traffic, and three lighthouses have been built to protect shipping. The original two worked as a pair from 1716, and they were replaced in 1906 by the current one.
   From Roman times, beacon fires were lit to

warn ships of the danger of the Bill. A petition to Trinity House was put forward for a lighthouse in the early 18th century, but Trinity House opposed it. They later conceded that a lighthouse was needed, and George I granted the patent on 26 May 1716. Trinity House issued a lease to William Barrett and Francis Browne to build and maintain one or more lighthouses.

With the help of a generous grant from its Maritime Charity, Trinity House has renovated the Visitor Centre at Portland Bill Lighthouse. Opened to the public on 29 March 2015, the impressive main exhibit allows you to learn about the lighthouse and its keepers and find out about Trinity House, the organisation that operates the lighthouse and has safeguard the mariner for over 500 years. The exhibition contains a number of interactive displays and historical artefacts and offers the opportunity to encounter a stormy sea journey in the exhilarating zone 'Into The Dark'.

In 2019, Portland Bill Lighthouse underwent a modernisation project, and the character and range of the main navigation light were changed, decreasing from 25 to 18 Nautical Miles. New LED lanterns were installed, and the rotating optic was relocated and placed on display at the base of the tower.

If you are planning to arrive at the centre

Tell them Purdey sent you…

towards the end of the day we would advise calling the lighthouse on 01305 821050 prior to arrival to confirm the final tour time and remaining availability.

Visitor Centre only
Adults £3.00
Family ticket (2 adults and up to 2 children) £7.00
Child (age 16 and under and accompanied by a paying Adult - max 4 children per adult).
Please note minimum height restriction of
1.1 metres tall to climb the tower £1.50
Concession £2.50

Visitor Centre and Lighthouse
Adults £8.50
Family ticket (2 adults and up to 2 children) £25.00
Child (age 16 & under)
Please note minimum height restriction of
1.1 metres tall to climb the tower £6.50
Concession £7.50

Portland Bill Lighthouse Visitor Centre accepts both cash and card payments.

Please note, Trinity House reserves the right to close for operational reasons at short notice.
Monday – Sunday   10:00 - 17:00

FANTASY ISLAND

Bowleaze Coveway, Weymouth   DT3 6PW
                                    01305 834746

www.fantasyislandweymouth.co.uk

Tell them Purdey sent you…

www.facebook.com/FantasyIslandWeymouth/
info@fantasyislandweymouth.co.uk

Free Entry. Ride Token Deals. 13 Rides, Big Top Games, Ghost Train (£.2.50), Outdoor Funfair, Indoor Funhouse, Arcade Gaming, Outdoor seating, Car Parking, Baby Facilities, Birthday Parties. Sunset Restaurant & Licensed Coffee Bar.

3 Hour Wristband (Over 3yrs) £15.99
1.5 Hour Wristband (Under 3yrs Only) £6.99
Monday - Sunday   10am – 10pm.

THE KEEP MILITARY MUSEUM

Barrack Road, Dorchester,   DT1 1RN
                                  01305 264066

www.keepmilitarymuseum.org

The regimental museum of The Devonshire and Dorset Regiment and Dorset Yeomanry. 400 years of local military history. Children's

Tell them Purdey sent you…

trails, hands-on activities, dress-up and other activities. First World War Trench experience.

Adults	£7.50
Seniors (over 65s)	£6.00
Students	£4.50
Children	£3.00
Under 5s	FREE
Family (2 adults 3 children)	£18.00

Monday – Saturday	10:00 - 17:00
Sunday	CLOSED

DINOSAUR MUSEUM

https://www.thedinosaurmuseum.com/
Icen Way, Dorchester, Dorset   DT1 1EW
01305 269880
Admission desk & info etc: 01305 269880

Tell them Purdey sent you…

Administration & Press Office: 01305 269741
info@thedinosaurmuseum.com

Hear the sounds and even smell the breath of a T-Rex as you explore Jurassic Dorset. Learn from the pioneers of fossil discovery including Mary Anning and Richard Owen and explore the rich dinosaur heritage of the Jurassic coast by seeing and touching our real fossil displays including dinosaur heads, teeth, eggs and even Poo!

Make your own dinosaur discoveries in our excavation pit, solve dinosaur puzzles and dare to put your hand in a feely box! Dinosaurs even come to the forefront of technology.

Enhance your visit with free fun sheets to win a Dino Hunters Achievement Certificate and explore our gift shop for that perfect dinosaur gift including fossils, models, clothing and books.

Adults	£13.00
Children	£9.00
Children under 3	FREE
Monday - Friday	09:00 - 17:00
Saturday	CLOSED
Sunday	CLOSED

Tell them Purdey sent you…

TUTANKHAMUN EXHIBITION

www.tutankhamun-exhibition.co.uk/
High West Street, Dorchester, Dorset DT1 1UW
Telephone: 01305 269 571
info@tutankhamun-exhibition.co.uk

A spectacular recreation of Tutankhamun's tomb and treasures. This internationally acclaimed exhibition spans time itself. Extensively featured on television throughout the world. Full school service plus specialist Egyptian shop including books.

Adults	£16.00
Children	£11.00
Children under 5	FREE

Tell them Purdey sent you…

Monday - Sunday   10am – 4pm

WINTER OPENING TIMES
1st November until Easter
Open Every Weekend and School Holidays
10am – 4pm

TEDDY BEAR MUSEUM

Eastgate, corner of High East St. & Salisbury St,
Dorchester Dorset   DT1 1JU
                             01305 266040

info@teddybearmuseum.co.uk
www.teddybearmuseum.co.uk/

Tell them Purdey sent you…

www.facebook.com/teddybearmuseumdorch/
The Teddy Bear Museum's ever-growing collections of teddy bears encompass bears from the very earliest to modern favourites. From antique and vintage bears dating from as early as 1906 to individually crafted designer bears by internationally renowned artists of the late 20th century.
Prices not shown

Monday - Sunday   10:00 - 16:00

MAX GATE

Hardy's House, Max Gate
Atmospheric Victorian home designed by Thomas Hardy
Alington Avenue, Dorchester, Dorset, DT1 2FN

Tell them Purdey sent you…

Hardy's House, Max Gate, an austere but sophisticated town house a short walk from the town centre of Dorchester, was the home of Dorset's most famous author and poet Thomas Hardy. Hardy, who designed the house in 1885, wanted to show that he was part of the wealthy middle classes of the area, to reflect his position as a successful writer, and to enable him to enter polite society. The house was named after a nearby tollgate keeper called Henry Mack. The tollgate was known locally as 'Mack's Gate', which Hardy then used with a different spelling when he named his house, 'Max Gate'.

Many of Hardy's possessions were dispersed before we acquired the house, but we've furnished the rooms for you to enjoy the spaces he created to write and live in. He wrote some of his most famous novels here, including Tess of the d'Urbervilles and Jude the Obscure, as well as much of his poetry.

You will find the garden much as it was originally planned, with high walls and large trees encircling the property to preserve Hardy's privacy. The sundial, designed by Hardy, was erected by his late wife, Florence, in his memory.

2024

Ticket type	Gift aid	Standard
Adult	£11.00	£10.00
Child	£5.50	£5.00
Family	£27.50	£25.00

Tell them Purdey sent you…

1 adult + up to 3 children   £16.50   £15.00

Monday   CLOSED
House/Garden   10:30 - 16:30
Last entry one hour before closing.

DORSET MUSEUM
01305 262735

High West Street, Dorchester DT1 1XA
www.dorsetmuseum.org/
www.facebook.com/dorsetmuseum/
enquiries@dorsetmuseum.org

The Museum began by collecting natural history and archaeology.

Literature, fine art, textiles, costume, local history, and photography collections grew over time. The Thomas Hardy collection was a major bequest in 1937.

Today the Museum looks after an incredible four million objects.

10% discount for Adult and Young Person Unlimited Ticket booked online using discount code DM01

Dorset Museum & Art Gallery Entry
(Includes Unlimited Entry for One Year)
Adult   £14.00
Concession   £11.00
Child with Adult   FREE
Carer with Disabled Person   FREE
Monday – Sunday   10.00 - 5.00

Tell them Purdey sent you…

TASTE Café

Monday – Saturday 9.00 - 4.00
Sunday 10:00 - 4:00

HARDY'S MONUMENT

www.nationaltrust.org.uk/visit/dorset/hardy-monument

Monument to Vice-Admiral Hardy
Black Down, Portesham, Dorset, DT2 9HY

The Hardy Monument (sometimes referred to as Hardy's Monument) is a 72-foot-high (22 m) monument on the summit of Black Down in Dorset, erected in 1844 by public subscription in memory of Vice Admiral Sir Thomas Hardy, flag captain of Admiral Lord Nelson at the Battle of Trafalgar.

Admiral Hardy lived in Portesham and his family owned the Portesham estate which stretched from the middle of Portesham to Black Down. The site for the monument was chosen because the Hardy family wanted a monument which could be used as a landmark for shipping. The monument has been shown on navigational charts since 1846 and is visible from a distance of 60 miles (97 km).

The monument is situated on Black Down, a hill overlooking the English Channel near

Tell them Purdey sent you…

Portesham in Dorset, England, on the road between Abbotsbury and Martinstown. It was restored in 1900 by his descendants and bought in 1938 by the National Trust for the sum of £15.

The monument was designed to look like a spyglass, as Admiral Hardy would have used on board ship. Its eight corners are aligned with the compass points. Viewed from the ground the corner to the right of the lightning conductor points due south. The benchmark on the northwest face denotes the altitude of Black Down at 780 feet (240 m).

Monument Tour

Ticket type	Gift aid	Standard
Adult	£4.40	£4.00
Child	£2.20	£2.00
Monday		CLOSED
Tuesday		CLOSED
Wednesday - Sunday		11:00 - 16:00

DORSET FALCONRY PARK

01305 250710

www.dorsetfalconrypark.com/

Husband and wife team Martin and Tara Ballam opened Dorset Falconry Park in 2019.

Martin has worked in the industry for over 40 years and has worked in many collections.

Tell them Purdey sent you…

His own journey began with Xtreme Falconry, an off site display team and experience day company. However his passion was always to follow his dream of conservation and that is when Dorset Falconry Park was opened and home to the birds in his collection.

Tara is a qualified secondary school science teacher with a degree in Zoology and has supported Martin with his passion and dream. Tara enjoys promoting the educational aspect of the work done here.

Philip, Connie and Elsie (their three children) are always busy at the park too. Philip is always behind the scenes whilst the girls are following in their dad's footsteps to promote the conservation and education of raptors.

VIP Family Session

£149 (up to 4 people) Exclusive falconry experience with Hawks, Falcons and Owls for 2 adults and 2 children. Please allow approximately one and a half hours for this experience
Additional family members may join the group to take part, £20 per person.
This is suitable for ages 6/7 years and upwards

Owl Encounter

£75 per person
We all love owls and you can meet them, hold

Tell them Purdey sent you…

them and fly them! Barn Owls, Tawny Owls and Eagle owls to name but a few. Experience the thrill of getting up close and personal with the most magical of all birds of prey. A truly unforgettable experience.

Suitable for ages 14 years upwards (14-16 year olds must have a spectating adult accompany them)

Ultimate Experience

£125 per person

After an introduction to your instructor and the birds you will experience flying hawks and owls to the glove and have the opportunity to handle an Eagle. This really is an ultimate gift experience. Please allow approximately one and a half hours for this experience.

Suitable for ages 14 years upwards (14-16 year olds must have a spectating adult accompany)

| Monday - Wednesday | CLOSED |
| Thursday - Sunday | 10am - 5pm |

HARDY'S COTTAGE

www.nationaltrust.org.uk/visit/dorset/hardys-cottage

Evocative cob and thatch cottage - birthplace of Thomas Hardy

Higher Bockhampton, near Dorchester, Dorset, DT2 8QJ

Thomas Hardy's Cottage, in Higher

Tell them Purdey sent you...

Bockhampton, Dorset, is a small cob and thatch building that is the birthplace of the English author Thomas Hardy. He was born there in 1840 and lived in the cottage until he was aged 34—during which time he wrote the novels Under the Greenwood Tree (1872) and Far from the Madding Crowd (1874)—when he left home to be married to Emma Gifford.

The cottage was built by Hardy's great-grandfather in 1800. It is now a National Trust property, and a popular tourist attraction. The property has a typical cottage garden, and the interior displays furniture which, although not from the Hardy family, is original to the period. The property is situated on the northern boundary of Thorncombe Wood. It is only three miles from Max Gate, the house that Hardy designed and lived in with Emma Gifford from 1885 until his death in 1928.

The cottage was given listed building status in 1956 and is listed Grade II the National Heritage List for England.

In 2012 the go ahead was given to a project to build a new visitor centre near the cottage. The project also included new trails in Thorncombe Wood. The project, which secured £525,000 from the Heritage Lottery Fund, was a joint partnership between Dorset County Council and the National Trust. The visitor centre opened in September 2014.

Tell them Purdey sent you…

Ticket type	Gift aid	Standard
Adult	£11.00	£10.00
Child	£5.50	£5.00
Family	£27.50	£25.00
1 adult + up to 3 children	£16.50	£15.00

https://www.nationaltrust.org.uk/visit/dorset/hardys-cottage#place-opening-times

FRANK'S GARDEN
PRESTON
HTTPS://WWW.FACEBOOK.COM/PAGES/FRANKS-GARDEN-PRESTON-WEYMOUTH/102271428281954

Tell them Purdey sent you…

CAR PARKING

You may be lucky enough to find a free parking space but these are for an hour and be careful as the Traffic Wardens are active.

There are some spaces along the Harbourside.

STANDARD CHARGES

1st April – 31st October

Half Hour	£1.50
1 Hour	£3.00
2 Hours	£4.50
3 Hours	£6.00
4 Hours	£7.50
10 Hours	£15.00

Monday – Sunday 6pm – 8pm Free
Electric Vehicle Charging:
Normal Parking Charges Apply
Disabled Charges Apply (Plus 1 Hour)

SWANNERY CAR PARK

Radipole Park Drive
DT4 7TY
915 Spaces, 18 Disabled, 3 Motorcycle
Pay by Card, Cash, Online/App Phone
JustPark 6204

Swannery Carpark is reverting to Winter Prices!

Tell them Purdey sent you…

BEACH CAR PARK

Preston Road, Weymouth DT4 7SX
281 spaces | 0 disabled | 0 motorcycle
Pay by Cash Card Phone Online / App
JustPark location no. 6202
Height restriction: 2.1

PAVILION CAR PARK

Weymouth Pavilion, The Esplanade, DT4 8DZ
01305 783225
318 spaces | 14 disabled | 1 motorcycle
Pay by Cash Card Phone Online / App
JustPark location no. 6200
Height restriction: No restriction

WEYMOUTH RAILWAY STATION CAR PARK

Located at King Street, Weymouth, DT4 7BN.
Offers 51 spaces.
Pricing:

Mon-Fri (All day):	£13.50
(Fri in after 00:00, Tue out by 04:00) flat rate of	£4.50
(in after 12:00, out by 00:00)	
	£9.00
(in 00:00-12:00, out by 00:00).	
Sat-Sun (All day 24 hours)	£4.50

Tell them Purdey sent you…

(ends at 00:00).
Weekly: £35.90
Monthly: £126.70
Quarterly: £380.10
Yearly: £1267

Payment options: Pay and display, cards, cash, contactless.
Blue Badge holders must register with South Western Railway for free parking.
Reviews mention some challenges with payment methods.

OVERCOMBE CAR PARK

Heron Close, Weymouth DT3 6SX
180 spaces | 0 disabled | 0 motorcycle
Pay by Cash Card Phone Online / App
JustPark location no. 6201

WEYMOUTH MOUNT PLEASANT CAR PARK

Mercery Road, Weymouth DT3 5HJ
Weymouth park and ride
1,000 spaces | 12 disabled | 20 motorcycle
Free

HARBOURSIDE CAR PARK

Commercial Road, Weymouth DT4 8NG
94 spaces | 6 disabled | 2 motorcycle
Pay by Card Cash Online / App Phone

Tell them Purdey sent you…

JustPark location no. 6222

GOVERNOR'S LANE CAR PARK
16 East St. Weymouth. DT4 8BW.
60 spaces | 4 disabled | 1 motorcycle
Pay by Card Cash Online / App Phone
JustPark location no. 6213

PARK STREET CAR PARK
Reopens August
162 spaces | 10 disabled | 1 motorcycle
Pay by Cash Phone Online / App Card
JustPark location no. 6221
Postcode for sat nav: DT4 7DQ

ROYAL YARD CAR PARK
31 spaces | 2 disabled | 0 motorcycle
Pay by Cash Phone Online / App Card
JustPark location no. 6223
Postcode for sat nav: DT4 7DA

NOTHE CAR PARK
196 spaces | 9 disabled | 3 motorcycle
Pay by Cash Phone Online / App Card
JustPark location no. 6208
Postcode for sat nav: DT4 8UD
Charges apply Monday to Sunday 8am to 6pm
Up to 30 mins   50p
Up to 1 hour   £1.00

Tell them Purdey sent you…

Up to 2 hours	£1.50
Up to 3 hours	£2.20
Up to 4 hours	£3.50
Up to 10 hours	£6.00

Monday to Sunday 6pm to 8am: Free

LODMOOR CAR PARK
565 spaces | 15 disabled | 7 motorcycle
Pay by Cash Card Phone Online / App
JustPark location no. 6203
Postcode for sat nav: DT4 7SX

FISHING

For years visitors to Weymouth and the surrounding areas have enjoyed hunting for the fish which swim around these shores.

Weymouth is accredited with having the largest professional fleet of fishing vessels operating out of a British Harbour.

Just a short trip from shore are the famous fishing grounds of the Shambles and Adamant sandbanks.

Inshore fishing offers Ray, Conger Eel, Bull Huss, Gurnards, Tope and Smoothounds.

Some of the best sea fishing in the country is available.

From Weymouth Beach you can possibly catch Sea Bass, Pollock, Whiting, Pout and Grey Mullet.

From Chesil Beach with feathers you can catch Mackerel and from the Stone and Pleasure Pier possibly Sea Bass and even the possibility of squid.

In the Harbour many a young person has

Tell them Purdey sent you…

enjoyed dropping the crab lines and catching crabs. It is also possible to catch Silver Eels.

FISHING TACKLE

Weymouth Angling Centre was opened in 1996 by Andy and Charlotte Selby. Over the last 20 years the business has built a reputation of offering an extensive range of sea angling products, alongside trusted advice and knowledge from friendly local staff.

WEYMOUTH ANGLING CENTRE
2 St Edmunds Street
Weymouth
Dorset
DT4 8AR
01305777771
wac@weymouthangling.com
www.weymouthangling.com/

TYPES OF FISH

BALLAN WRASSE, EUROPEAN SEABASS, EUROPEAN CONGAR, CORKWING WRASSE, ATLANTIC MACKEREL, POUTING, WHITING, POLLACK, BREAM, PLAICE, TURBOT

Tell them Purdey sent you…

PLACES TO FISH

FISHING SITES CLOSE TO WEYMOUTH

Forecast for Fishing:
https://tides4fishing.com/uk/england/weymouth/forecast/fishing

LOCAL FISHING INFORMATION
www.weymouthangling.com/products/Local-Fishing-Information-c147407953

Tell them Purdey sent you…

SHOPS IN WEYMOUTH

The shops are in the order we passed them on our way into Weymouth and a walk around Weymouth so they are listed road by road.

LYNCH LANE

OTTOMAN KEBAB HOUSE
01305 788812

9 Lynch Lane
www.ottomankebabhouse.com/

Haven Owners 10% discount

Kebabs, Pizza, Jacket Potatoes etc.

We have had a few take aways from here. The 10% Haven Owner discount is welcome and they serve good sized portions and are welcoming.

Tell them Purdey sent you…

BELLE'S TRADITIONAL BAKERS

www.facebook.com/BellesTraditionalBakers/

Take away pies, sausage rolls etc.

Monday – Wednesday	CLOSED
Thursday	09:30 - 15:30
Friday	09:30 - 15:30
Saturday	09:00 - 16:00
Sunday	10:00 - 15:30

WISE BUYS   07812 349792

www.facebook.com/wisebuysweymouth/

Hundreds of bargain branded food products. We stock a mixture of in date, Short dated & best before date expired products.

| Monday – Saturday | 09:00 - 17:00 |
| Sunday | 10:00 - 16:00 |

Haven Owners 10% discount

Purdey and I have shopped here on many occasions as they sell a good selection of dog treats. Their stock is low priced, much of it is close to sell by date or past the date, hence the price. There is a limited amount of alcohol and household cleaners etc. Friendly people!

Tell them Purdey sent you…

THE MUNCH BOX 07588 729175

www.facebook.com/munchboxweymouth
Munchboxweymouth@outlook.com

Tuesday – Friday   8.15 – 2.30pm

Local and good quality produce is used, and they serve a good coffee and their tea is only £1!

MENU FOOD & DRINK

Breakfast	Roll	Torpedo
3 free range egg	£2.70	£2.70
Bacon	£3.00	£3.40
Sausage	£3.00	£3.40
Sausage & Bacon	£3.60	£4.00
Bacon & Egg	£3.30	£3.80
Sausage & Egg	£3.30	£3.80
Sausage, Bacon & Egg	£4.00	£4.60
Bacon, Lettuce & Tomato	£3.30	£3.60

Burgers	
1/4 lb Beef Burger	£2.80
1/4 lb Cheese Burger	£3.40
1/4 lb Bacon Burger	£3.60
1/4 lb Egg & Cheese Burger	£3.70
1/4 lb Cheese & Bacon Burger	£4.00
1/4 lb Egg & Bacon Burger	£4.00

Add an extra burger or Chips for 50p
Upgrade your cheese to spicy or smoked Cheese for 50p
Add Gherkins to any burger for FREE

Small Breakfast Wrap - £4
Sausage, 2 Bacon, Hashbrown & Egg
Large Breakfast Wrap - £6
2 Sausage, 3 Bacon, 2 Hashbrowns & 2 Eggs
Small Breakfast Box - £4.50
Sausage, Bacon, Egg, Hashbrown, Beans & Buttered Roll
Large Breakfast Box - £6.50
2 Sausage, 2 Bacon, 2 Eggs, 2 Hashbrowns, Beans & Buttered Roll

Chicken - Plain or Spicy
Chicken wrap - Chicken, Bacon, Cheese, Salad & Mayo £4.50
Chicken Burger with Cheese £4.00
Chicken, Bacon & Cheese Burger £4.70
Add an extra chicken burger for £1.50

Munch Burger - £6.50
1/2 lb burger, 2 bacon, 2 sausage, egg, cheese & onion
Breakfast Burger - £6.50
1/4 lb burger, 2 sausage, 2 hashbrowns, mushrooms, egg & cheese
Farmyard Burger - £6.50
1/4 lb burger, chicken, 2 bacon, egg & cheese
Miss Piggy Burger - £6.50
1/4 lb burger, 2 bacon, pulled pork, cheese, 3 beer battered onion rings & BBQ sauce
Chicken Stack Burger - £6.80
Chicken, 2 bacon, 2 hashbrowns, cheese
The Hot Chuck - £4.50
Salad jalapenos, spicy, hot, chicken, mexican, spicy cheese, spicy mayo
The Hot One - £6.50
1/4 lb burger, spicy chicken, 2 bacon, cheese, jalapenos & hot sauce

Americano	£1.45
Flat White	£1.70
Latte	£1.70
Cappuccino	£1.70
Espresso	£1.45
Double Espresso	£1.55
Mocha	£1.70
Hot Chocolate	£1.70
Decaf Americano	£1.45
Monin Syrup	40p
Tea	£1.00
Decaf Tea	£1.20
Flavoured Tea	£1.35
Bottled Water	85p
Cans	£1

Snacks
Chocolate Bars 80p
Crisps 80p
Flapjacks 90p

10% DISCOUNT AVAILABLE
BLUE LIGHT CARD

Extras
Free Range Eggs	50p
Mature Cheese	50p
Mushrooms	50p
Sausage	60p
2 Bacon	£1.20
2 Hashbrowns	£1
Black pudding	60p
6 Battered Onion Rings	£1.80

Chips £2.50
Cheesy Chips £3.50
Sausage & Chips £4.00
4 Southern fried Chicken strips & Chips £4.50
8 Pigs in blankets & Chips £4.50
(not just for Christmas)

Tell them Purdey sent you…

TIKKA TRAK

Curry Van   07843199781

www.facebook.com/TikkaTrak/
info@tikkatrak.co.uk
Wednesday   1pm – 8pm

THE GARDENER'S RETREAT

01305 759503

THOMPSONS
info@gardenersretreat.com
www.facebook.com/gardenersretreat
Monday – Sunday   9am – 3pm

HI TECH DRY CLEANERS

LANEHOUSE ROCKS RD

SEARGEANT BUNS BAKERY

www.sgtbun.com
https://www.facebook.com/people/Sgt-Bun-Bakery/100070254964398/

LYNCH ROAD

ONE STOP CONVENIENCE STORE

(7 days, 7-10pm)

Tell them Purdey sent you…

ALF'S FISH & CHIPS
01305 783342

www.alfsfishandchips.com/
www.alfsfishandchips.com/menus

Established in 1955 by Alfonzo, Alf's Fish & Chip Shop has kept its name to this day.

In September 2015, the Graham family became the latest owners to continue and improve on the high standard of food the locals and holiday makers love to enjoy.

Monday, Tuesday & Wednesday	4pm to 9pm
Thursday & Friday	11:30 - 2pm
	4pm to 9pm
Saturday	11:30 to 9pm
Sunday	CLOSED

We have enjoyed their fish and chips on a few occasions. There is parking and they serve quickly. There are seats to sit and wait for your food.

CHICKERELL RD

CO-OPERATIVE SUPERMARKET
Monday – Sunday   6.30 – 22.00
NOT DOG FRIENDLY

Tell them Purdey sent you…

THE ADMIRAL HARDY PUB

01305 784754

www.admiralhardypub.co.uk/
www.facebook.com/pages/The-Admiral-Hardy-Pub-Weymouth/542904869066250

We stock a fantastic selection of drinks - no matter what your tipple, there'll be something for you. Choose from smooth draught lagers, craft beers, ciders, wine, cocktails and soft drinks. Come and join us for a drink.

Get your sports fix at Admiral Hardy; watch Sky Sports on our big screen or one of the four large TVs around the bar. There's plenty more to keep you entertained, including darts, two pool tables and a family room. Enjoy your drink in our beer garden, when the sun is shining.

Food is served from noon. Whether you're stopping by for lunch or dinner, you'll find all your favourite pub classics - fish and chips, lasagne, grills, burgers and more!

Enjoy free parking at Admiral Hardy. The team are looking forward to welcoming you.

ABBOTSBURY ROAD

SUE RYDER CHARITY SHOP
NOT DOG FRIENDLY

Tell them Purdey sent you…

GOLDEN KITCHEN
Chinese Take Away

WELL PHARMACY 01305 786787
www.finder.well.co.uk/store/weymouth-abbotsbury-road

Monday - Friday   09:00 - 18:00
Saturday & Sunday   CLOSED

LONDIS & POST OFFICE
                         01305 787571
Monday – Sunday   0700 – 2200

DORSET KEBAB HOUSE
No reviews or visible phone number

HEL'S KITCHEN 01305 770021
Hel's Kitchen is run by Helen, who had over 30 years experience in Chinese takeaway catering. Helen was the first Chinese takeaway providing delivery service through Weymouth.

WAVERLEY ARMS (The Nest Café)
www.thenestweymouth.co.uk/

We are a small team of mostly volunteers,

Tell them Purdey sent you…

keen to work together with our local community, businesses, faith groups and anyone passionate about reducing food waste, addressing food poverty and eating healthily. The Nest Weymouth CIC is a Christian organisation with these values at its heart. We have 3 Directors, Neil Hardisty, Nigel Ovenden and Elaine Pullen, who oversee the project and make decisions about its running and future direction. We also have a full time manager, Stacey Wilkinson (pictured below), who currently runs the shop on a day to day basis.

THE BLUSHING BUDDHA HAIR & BEAUTY
www.facebook.com/euphoriabeautytherapysalon/

MACEYS
CONVENIENCE STORE

07479 020879

www.facebook.com/maceysshop/

WEYMOUTH VAPE

01305 761445

www.weymouthvape.co.uk/
www.facebook.com/weymouthvape
Blue Light Discount 10%
Prison Workers Discount 10%

Tell them Purdey sent you…

FACIAL ATTRACTION

01305 773363

www.facebook.com/weymouthbeautysalon

GIMBLETT HARDWARE

01305 786444

Disabled friendly, no step.

Good prices. They cut keys, have dog treats, hardware, gardening, kitchenware, tools and parking outside.

Very welcoming and Purdey loved her dog treats!

SON OF ABACUS
FURNITURE & STUFF

01305 777966

www.sonofabacus.co.uk/

I'm in the shop on Fridays and Saturdays, and other times by appointment.

I have been selling furniture as Abacus here on Abbotsbury Road since 1988, in partnership, as a sole trader, as a limited company, and now as Son of Abacus.

These days I am the whole shebang and split my time between shop and workshop.

Tell them Purdey sent you…

THE ROCK
PUB   01305 777797

www.therockweymouth.co.uk
www.facebook.com/pages/The-Rock-Weymouth/224180087609614

Saturday: 12:00 - 01:00
Sunday: 00:00 - 01:00
                                   12:00 - 20:00

PREMIER
CONVENIENCE STORE

SPOT
St Pauls CHARITY SHOP

                                   01305 750951
Monday – Friday   1000 – 1600

www.stpaulsweymouth.org/help/spot
www.facebook.com/StPaulsOuTreach/

Run by friendly volunteers. Purdey and I love visiting this shop and you never know what you are going to find to buy. There is parking in the church.

St Paul's Church is a peaceful retreat and the Parish Centre Parish Hall is available for hire by clubs, organisations and individuals Mondays to Saturdays on a regular of one off basis subject to availability. They have a small meeting room which accommodates up to fifteen people, the main hall can hold up to a hundred people. Their well equipped kitchen can be used with prior arrangement. There is a small cloister garden

Tell them Purdey sent you…

which can be used during the summer. The car park is free and reserved for church, hall and charity shop users. 01305 771 217. stpweymouth@gmail.com. Why not drop by the charity shop and say hello to the lovely ladies and gents who work there.

ABLE CABS 01305 334455
Accessibility Taxis
www.ablecabs.co.uk/

Dogs are welcome in the office but knock on the window first as they have a dog of their own.

FAMILY SHOPPER 01269 594300
www.familyshopperstores.co.uk/

All Family Shopper stores are locally owned by independent retailers… With over 80 stores you can be sure there's a Family Shopper at the heart of your local community.

MORGAN BROWN
HAIR & BEAUTY

01305 788290

www.morganbrownhairandbeautyweymouth.co.uk

Visit your one-stop department store for hair and beauty! We provide different areas/mini businesses for lashes, nails, hair, facials,

Tell them Purdey sent you…

eyebrows, massage, and much more. Our ethos is to provide a one stop sanctuary for hair and beauty treatments, housing the very best professionals in their chosen field.

JOY WOK CHINESE TAKE AWAY
01305 789288

www.joywokweymouth.co.uk
www.facebook.com/p/Joy-Wok-100069310911835/

Monday – Sunday   17:00 - 22:45

RAPID MOBILITY 01305 759800

www.rapidmobilityltd.com

Rapid Mobility supplies a wide variety of high-quality mobility products such as scooters, wheelchairs, electric beds and all other disability equipment.

Monday - Friday   0900 – 1700
Saturday   09:00 - 16:00
Sunday   CLOSED

WEYMOUTH PHARMACY
01305 785754

www.nhs.uk/services/pharmacy/weymouth-pharmacy/FPN51

Monday – Friday   09:00 - 18:00
   Saturday   CLOSED
   Sunday   CLOSED

Tell them Purdey sent you…

SWEET KITCHEN 01305 602542
www.sweetkitchenonline.co.uk
Monday – Sunday   17:00 - 22:00

RAY'S CHICKEN 01305 783333
www.rays-chicken.co.uk
Monday – Sunday   16:00 - 22:30

CAFÉ INDIA   01305 839330
www.weymouthcafeindia.co.uk
Tuesday - Sunday   17:00 - 21:00
Monday   CLOSED

NO ALCOHOL

FLORAL COUTURE by JAY
01305 773940
www.floralcouturebyjay.co.uk
www.facebook.com/floralcouturebyjay
Monday, Tuesday,
Thursday, Friday   08:30 - 17:00
Wednesday   08:30 - 15:00
Saturday   8:30 – 13:00
Sunday   CLOSED

Tell them Purdey sent you…

WESSEX LOCKSMITHS

01305 761047

www.wessexlocksmiths.co.uk

Monday - Friday   08:30 - 17:30
Saturday & Sunday   CLOSED

WESTHAM ROAD

THE SALVATION ARMY
CHARITY SHOP

MARRIA'S CAFÉ   07876 735176

www.facebook.com/profile.php?id=10006923796887

English cafe with a touch of Chinese, Full English breakfast, coffees, teas, hot chocolate, Chinese teas, speciality teas, Takeaway sandwiches, bacon baps, omelettes etc.

Monday – Sunday   08:00 - 17:00

SURPLUS INTERNATIONAL

01305 786600

www.facebook.com/groups/603509643017981/

www.bsaguns.co.uk/

Tell them Purdey sent you…

Military, bits of airsoft and firearms.

Tuesday	0900 – 1700
Wednesday – Monday	10.30 - 1630
Sunday	CLOSED

NOSTALGIA UNLIMITED
01305 768315

www.facebook.com/people/Lazer-Keys-Nostalgia-Unlimited/100057326654698/

We provide cheap and reliable key cutting starting from £5, watch batteries from £5 and watch straps from £6 along with DVD's, CD's and vinyl from £1. We also sell vintage toys, cards and collectables from 50p all in a family and pet friendly environment.

Monday – Friday	10:00 - 16:00
Saturday	10:00 - 17:00
Sunday	CLOSED

Blue Light Discount 10%

An amazing Aladdin's Cave of videos, gaming books, collectables and other things. Set aside time, there is a lot to look at. The owner is friendly and helpful.

CRAFTLINES
01305 767302

4 Westham Road   CRAFT SHOP

www.facebook.com/people/Craftlines-Weymouth/100063580960079/

Tell them Purdey sent you…

craftlinesweymouth@gmail.com

Wool, needles, sewing equipment, inspiration, and a welcoming greeting.

Monday – Saturday   10:00 - 16:00
Sunday   CLOSED

Craft Group Monday and Friday 11am – 1pm £1 no need to book. Teacher Present: Crochet & Knitting

A very well stocked wool and craft shop. You will be assured of an enthusiastic welcome and advice if you need it. Be sure to take a look at the window display of amazing knifing and crafting skills which follows a theme which is either relevant to an event or a theme chosen. They also sell some of the creations from the window when the "exhibition" is over. There are also items made by local people for sale in the shop.

SO N SEWS   01305 766411

www.sonsews.co.uk/#/
www.facebook.com/sonsews

So 'n' Sews is a family run business in Weymouth, Dorset, offering a wide range of fabrics for dress making, home furnishings and craft.

We have a large selection of sewing accessories and haberdashery items, some of

Tell them Purdey sent you…

which are available on our online shop.

In addition to this we sell net curtains, Janome sewing and embroidery machines and have a curtain making service.

Monday – Saturday   10:00 - 15:00
Sunday   CLOSED

QUAYSIDE LEATHER
07977 753148

3 Westham Road, Weymouth DT4 8NP
www.facebook.com/quayside.leather/

Monday – Saturday   9.30 – 16.30

Handbags, Travel Goods, Purses and Wallets.

A friendly welcome and a whole host of temptations as there are some lovely handbags and shopping bags for sale all delightfully displayed to tempt you.

FINNS
01305 778098

www.finns-weymouth.co.uk/
www.facebook.com/finns.weymouth
NOT DOG FRIENDLY

The best national and local bands every weekend with tribute acts featured monthly. The "Gig-Guide" section of this site contains the gig listings for the coming month.

Finns boasts the best rock juke box on the South Coast. We play Indie, Rock, Punk, Metal and Goth - So there's something for everyone,

Tell them Purdey sent you...

just check it out!

Finns is open until 2am every night and if the live music, rockin' atmosphere and good beer is not enough for you then you can always display your talents on the pool table!

Monday – Sunday   Midday - 2AM

LY NAILS & BEAUTY
07894 546912

www.facebook.com/lynailsnbeauty/

WEYMOUTH KEBAB
01305 771616

www.weymouthkebab.co.uk/

Monday - Sunday   04:00 -11:59

GOOD TO GO   07813 167719

Good 2 Go offers a wide selection of lunch food, and you can order online for delivery or collection.

The home of the Hog in a Box.

Hog in a Bun.

Pie and Mash.

They also provide food for Suppers, Weddings and office lunches.

Hot and cold take away food. There are four chairs so you can eat in as well.

Purdey and I love visiting here and the Hog in a Box is very tasty. It comes with stuffing, apple sauce,

Tell them Purdey sent you…

crackling and gravy. It is nice to be able to sit and eat it although you could always take it to the beach which is only a short walk away.

LONDIS

SUBWAY

GREAT GEORGE ST.

EARTH & BEAUTY
07811 181101

www.earthandbeauty.co.uk/

THE COMBAT LAB
07749 515574

www.thecombatlab.co.uk/
www.facebook.com/thecombatlab/
Info@thecombatlab.co.uk

We are a family-friendly martial arts academy based in the town centre of Weymouth, Dorset. Offering a range of adults and kids programmes across Brazilian Jiu-Jitsu (BJJ), Submission Grappling, Mixed Martial Arts (MMA) and Muay Thai, we are sure to have a class which will suit everyone. Includes a café.

Tell them Purdey sent you…

JURASSIC
CARAVAN & CAMPING ACCESSORIES
www.facebook.com/jurassic2018/
jurassiccca@btinternet.com   07725 783168

Camping and caravanning accessories. Wholesale goods for Hotels etc.

Monday	9.00 – 17.00
Tuesday	CLOSED
Wednesday	9.00 – 17,00
Thursday	9.00 – 16.00
Friday	9.00 – 17.00
Saturday	9.00 – 16.00
Sunday	CLOSED

VAPE D'AMI   07376 135094

8 Great George Street   VAPES
Vape.dami@gmail.com
www.vapedami.co.uk/
www.facebook.com/vapedami/

An UK Electronic Cigarette, E-liquid & Accessories Supplier. Offering One To One Advice. Friendly and helpful even for a beginner.

A very atmospheric vape shop. The layout is very attractive and the back wall is quite a surprise.

FOODPLUS   01305 459435

Tell them Purdey sent you…

www.facebook.com/53greatgeorgestreet/
Monday – Sunday   09:00 - 21:00

MOUNTAIN BEAUTY
07763 717402

www.mountainbeauty.co.uk
www.facebook.com/mountainbeautyweymouth/

THYME OUT CAFÉ
01305 766668

www.facebook.com/pages/Thyme-Out-Cafe/173163316225918
Monday – Saturday   08:30 - 17:00
Sunday   CLOSED

LITTLE DUCKLINGS
www.facebook.com/groups/146177721448740/permalink/146182571448255/

We will be opening little ducklings in May and will be based at 5 George Street Weymouth.

When you shop at little ducklings the profits will be going back into the community. We are going to be supporting children's projects from clubs and groups to nurseries and school in Weymouth and Portland We want to help them with equipment, goods and resources.

We are a baby / children shop and take donations from clothes to cots pushchair etc....

⭐ holiday clubs

Tell them Purdey sent you...

⭐ youth clubs
⭐ kits for sports clubs dance groups
⭐ breakfast clubs
⭐ nurseries schools pre school

Must be based in Weymouth and Portland
For children under 18

GOOD AS GOLD

(Jewellery)   01305 783355
www.goodasgoldjewellers.com

Dorset's ethical experience in jewellery shopping! Handmade jewellery made from ethically sourced and recycled silver, gold, palladium and platinum.

All Jewellery is designed, made, repaired and refurbished in store. We specialise in repairs, bespoke one-off pieces, remodelling, replicating and commercial projects. We love using old and unworn jewellery and remodelling them into pieces that bring joy. We also take great pride in insurance replacements, replicating pieces that may have been lost or stolen from photos you provide. No matter what the occasion we can find or create the perfect piece of unique jewellery just for you.

We are a small traditional business based in Weymouth, Dorset. Our Master Goldsmith Daniel and his teamwork in the shop creating new pieces and repairing cherished ones whilst

Tell them Purdey sent you…

giving the customers a breakdown of the work that is needed, and the costs involved. Daniel Moran is a goldsmith with over 30 years of experience and has been recognised as a Fellow of the Institute of Professional Goldsmiths. He was trained by some of the country's finest goldsmiths, serving his apprenticeship in the world-famous Hatton Garden, and is now passing on his hard-earned skills to young goldsmiths within his team in order to maintain the highest of standards.

Tuesday–Friday:	9:00–17:00
Saturday:	10:00–17:00
Sunday–Monday:	CLOSED

WELDMAR HOSPICE TRUST

Charity Shop

01305 787825

Monday – Saturday	0900 – 1700
Sunday	CLOSED

BUGSY'S
BAR & BISTRO   07807 377728
www.facebook.com/people/Bugsys-Bar-Bistro/100040215444161/

Tell them Purdey sent you…

THE DOGHOUSE
MICRO PUB

01305 567134

www.facebook.com/TheDoghouseWeymouth/

www.weymouthmicropub.co.uk/

We specialise in real ale, real cider and a

Tell them Purdey sent you…

range of UK, American, Australian and European craft cans and bottles. We have at least 6-8 different casks on tap, up to 12 during the summer months! Watch out for some surprising casks!

You can choose a variety of traditional pub snacks including Pipers crisps, Gruntled pork scratchings, Twiglets and various nuts. We are an ideal place for chatting and drinking!

Monday:	CLOSED
Tuesday & Wednesday:	2 – 7pm
Thursday:	2 – 7pm
Friday & Saturday:	Noon - 10pm
Sunday:	CLOSED

ST THOMAS STREET

JD WETHERSPOONS
WILLIAM HENRY

01305 763730

www.jdwetherspoon.com/pubs/all-pubs/england/dorset/the-william-henry-weymouth

NOT DOG FRIENDLY

This was part of a terrace of 12 houses, built in 1834 in the gardens of Gloucester Lodge. It was owned by Prince William Henry, Duke of Gloucester, and brother of George III. The

Tell them Purdey sent you…

king's visits to the lodge turned Weymouth into a fashionable resort. Richard Bower, twice mayor of Weymouth, lived in these premises from the 1830s to the 1870s. From the 1920s until the 1970s, the building housed Forte's 'Soda and Milk Bar'.

HOWLEYS TOYMASTER & CANDY PLANET

01305 779255
5 Frederick Place   TOY SHOP
Friendly helpful staff and a well-stocked shop.
Toys, Models and Games.
www.howleys.co.uk/

www.facebook.com/HowleysToyshop

JACKSONS
FISH & CHIPS   01305 776583
www.jacksonsfishandchips.com
www.facebook.com/JacksonsFishandChipsWeymouth/

Take Away and Sit Down.
Military Discount 10%

Tell them Purdey sent you…

TILLEYS
Bicycles & Motor Cycles

01305 785672

www.tilleysmotorcycles.co.uk

Tilleys as a business have existed for over 100 years serving Weymouth & Portland plus Dorchester, Poole, Bournemouth and surrounding Dorset villages. We have been specialists in motorcycles for all that time.

We can even boast having sold Thomas Hardy, the famous writer, a bicycle and taught his wife to ride her cycle.

We pride ourselves on running a business with a one stop shop attitude.

Motorbikes, Bicycles, Accessories and Repairs. Training. Tyres, Oils and Spares. Helmets.

CHANGING GROOMS

01305 759898

www.facebook.com/cghairandbeauty/

Monday	CLOSED
Tuesday	09:00 - 17:00
Wednesday	CLOSED
Thursday	09:00 - 17:00
Friday	09:00 - 19:30
Saturday	09:00 - 17:30
Sunday	CLOSED

Tell them Purdey sent you…

COBURG PLACE

VAPETOWN   0333 772 2092
www.vapetown.co.uk/pages/vape-town-weymouth

THE BLUE IRIS GALLERY
07834 875640

www.facebook.com/Theblueirisgallery/

Souwestcollectables1@hotmail.com

Monday	CLOSED
Tuesday - Friday	09:00 - 15:00
Saturday	09:00 - 16:00
Sunday	CLOSED

We are a Gift Shop Craft Store plus Wedding Elements Accessories

The Edinburgh Pub
THE HOUSE OF SOUNDS
01305 786363

www.facebook.com/edinburghhouseofsounds/

Monday	CLOSED
Tuesday	12:00 - 23:00
Wednesday	12:00 - 23:00
Thursday	12:00 - 23:00

Tell them Purdey sent you…

Friday	12:00 - 01:00
Saturday	12:00 - 01:00
Sunday	16:00 - 22:30

MARGARET GREEN
ANIMAL RESCUE   CHARITY SHOP
01305 839201
weymouth@mgar.org.uk
www.margaretgreenanimalrescue.org.uk/weymouth

| Monday - Saturday | 09:00 - 17:00 |
| Sunday | 10:00 - 16:00 |

DRY DOCK
www.facebook.com/people/DryDock/100090104267253/
StayHappy@DryDock.org.uk

| Monday – Saturday | 09:00 - 21:00 |
| Sunday | 11:00 - 21:00 |

Weekly Events
Wellbeing & Spiritual
Andy's Man Club Monday 7.00pm – 9.00pm
Sisterhood Circle Tuesday 10.30am – 11.30am
Mental Health Social Group Thursday 1.00pm – 3.00pm
Reflexology Thursday 1.00pm – 3.00pm

Tell them Purdey sent you…

Oracle & Palm Reading Thursday
1.30pm – 3.30pm

Support Groups
Housing Information Drop In
Thursday 10.00am – 1.00pm

Social Groups
Coffee & Crochet Wednesday 10.00am – 1pm
Pub Quiz Wednesday 7.00pm – 9.00pm
Boardgaming Thursday 6.00pm – 9.00pm
Knit & Natter Saturday 11.00am – 3.00pm
Conversation Club Sunday 4.00pm – 7.00pm

Music Events
Live Practices Tuesday 11.45am – 12.45pm
Community Choir Tuesday 2.00pm – 4.00pm
Beginner Guitar Course*
Tuesday 7.00pm – 8.00pm
Open Mic & Open Stage
Friday 6.00pm – 9.00pm
Live Bands Saturday 7.00pm – 9.00pm

WEYMOUTH CARDS
POST OFFICE

01305 789663

Monday - Friday	09:00 - 17:00
Saturday	09:00 - 13:00
Sunday	CLOSED

Tell them Purdey sent you…

MING WAH 01305 773282

www.mingwah.co.uk
www.facebook.com/MingWahChineseRestaurant/
Sunday   16:45 - 22:30
Monday   CLOSED
Tuesday - Friday   16:45 - 22:30

RONA
BAR & GRILL   01305 457190
www.ronabarandgrill.co.uk
Turkish Restaurant

ARTIST
NAILS & BEAUTY

01305 777751

www.facebook.com/artistnails/

Manicures, gel acrylic extensions, relaxing massages, lash treatment, brow treatments, waxing etc.. Certified Aw3 laser treatment centre, laser hair removal, tattoo removal, charcoal facials, wrinkle treatments.

Monday – Saturday   09:00 - 18:00
Sunday   CLOSED

SPECSAVERS   01305 761385
Monday – Friday   09:30 - 17:00
Saturday   08:30 - 17:00
Sunday   09:30 - 16:00

Tell them Purdey sent you…

ANDREW CARE
OPTICIANS

01305 777679

www.andrewcareopticians.co.uk
www.facebook.com/andrewcareweymouth/

We are a friendly independent partnership based on the South Coast of Dorset, established in 1986, we have been trading for over 30 years providing professional and affordable eyecare.

Monday - Friday	09:00 - 17:00
Saturday	CLOSED
Sunday	CLOSED

FINCA

01305 300400

COFFEE SHOP

www.facebook.com/fincaweymouth/

www.fincacoffee.co.uk/

Independent specialty coffee shop with a roastery at The Grove, Dorchester. Shops in Dorchester, Yeovil & Poundbury. Winner "Coffee Shop of the Year 2018" Dorset Food & Drink.

Monday – Saturday	8.00 – 17.00
Sunday	10.00 – 15.00

Tell them Purdey sent you...

BOOTS

W H SMITH

GRAPE TREE   01305 457130
www.grapetree.co.uk

Grape Tree is the UK's fastest growing name in healthier eating, bringing the finest natural whole foods at prices you can afford.

Monday - Saturday   09:00 - 17:00
Sunday   10:00 - 16:00

NAT WEST BANK

RANDOM COLLECTABLES
                          01305 781515
8-9 Bond Street   HOMEWARES

www.randomcollectables.co.uk
www.facebook.com/randomcollectables
Hello@randomcollectables.co.uk

Random Collectables want to bring quirky products to Dorset.

Shoes, Homeware, Accessories, Hats, Gloves.

Monday – Saturday   9.00 – 17.30
Sunday   10.00 – 16.00

Tell them Purdey sent you…

CAFÉ NERO

SANTANDER

BELLE'S
THE PINK CAKE SHOP
www.facebook.com/BellesTraditionalBakers/

WELDMAR HOSPICE
CHARITY SHOP

GEZZINI
BAR & RESTAURANT
www.facebook.com/p/Gezzini-Weymouth-61552419916277/

bananayouth77@gmail.com

Monday	CLOSED
Tuesday	CLOSED
Wednesday	00:00 - 22:00
Thursday	00:00 - 23:00
Friday	00:00 - 23:00
Saturday	00:00 - 23:00
Sunday	00:00 - 22:00

Tell them Purdey sent you…

RIEKER

www.rieker.co.uk/map/rieker-weymouth

The store stocks Rieker shoes for ladies and men, Remonte ladies shoes, handbags, slippers and shoecare. We also stock samples, end of line clearance and out of season footwear. You can come and save money on the latest season styles as well as the clearance bargains.

Monday - Friday	9:30 – 5:30
Saturdays	9:00 – 5:30
Sundays & Bank Holidays	11:00 – 4:00

what3words address: ///loses.scarcely.topic

CLARKS   01305 459380

69 St Thomas Street   SHOES
www.clarks.co.uk

Clarks are a British founded shoemakers, offering a selection of formal and casual footwear for men and women of all ages.

Monday – Saturday	09:00 - 17:30
Sunday	10:00 - 16:00

S W COAST

Refills   07958 260146
https://southwestcoast.co.uk/

Tell them Purdey sent you…

hello@southwestcoast.co.uk

South West Coast Refills is a small business on a big mission to make a positive impact to our environment and community on the Dorset South West Coast.

The SW Coast story began at our own kitchen table, out of frustration at being unable to find local packaging-free produce.

SW Coast began life as a market stall and accelerated and expanded into the small Weymouth shop. We added the online store selling items to make zero-waste an easy choice. We bring plastic free shopping to Weymouth & Portland.

We want to inspire our neighbours and wider community to make small changes towards a zero-waste lifestyle, learn and grow with us and believe in the difference they can make.

Summer 2019 passed in a bit of a blur of sunny market days, early starts, a HUGE amount of product research and some lovely beach sunsets. We flung ourselves into Autumn 2019 determined to find a permanent home (out of the rain!) for our zero waste shop.

We knew we wanted to be in Weymouth as Emma is passionate about seaside town regeneration and Weymouth as a town. We love living here and want to make plastic free

Tell them Purdey sent you…

shopping more accessible to everyone locally, giving them the choice to decide how they shop.

After a couple of shop premises slipped through the net and we got pipped to the post on more than one occasion, we were dejected and were beginning to wonder if we would have a home by Christmas.

But luck had our backs and proving that all good things come in small sizes, our perfect little shop became available. We signed the lease to 6 Coburg Place on October 18th and November passed in a flurry of sawdust and sanding!

Scroll on one year and we have moved from our little shop on the corner, expanded to a store which is lighter, brighter and infinitely bigger and better!

Our new shop is now packed to the brim full of products that you have requested: items we have sourced locally from local crafters and makers, ingredients you have deemed as store cupboard essentials as well as zero waste gifts and household items. Our Refill Station is ever popular and the number of people filling bottles increases daily!

We honestly believe that everyone, big or small can make a difference. Everything we do creates waste, however by becoming a conscious consumer you can choose to buy

Tell them Purdey sent you...

better, buy less, begin to understand supply chains, reconnect with food, support more local businesses and reduce consumer waste.

The brands we work with share our goal of working towards a greener future, by using only the most natural of ingredients and recyclable/biodegradable packaging.

Raise a reusable cup to SW Coast Refills! We hope you enjoy our little shop.   Rikki & Emma

VICTORIA ANN BRIDAL
01305 319359

www.victoriaannbridal.co.uk/

Located in the heart of the beautiful seaside town of Weymouth, Victoria Ann Bridal can boast being the only bridal shop in Weymouth, that can provide something special for every bride, mother of the bride and groom, bridesmaids, flower girls and the young ladies preparing for their prom.

You will always receive a warm and friendly reception from the first moment you walk through the door to the moment you walk down the aisle or arrive at your big occasion. All Victoria Ann Bridal's stunning collections including, Wedding Dresses, Bridesmaids Dresses, Mothers of the Bride and Groom's outfits, Flower girl Dresses, accessories and those all-important Prom Dresses are hand

Tell them Purdey sent you…

selected with care and love.

Victoria Ann Bridal's beautiful collections of dresses, outfits and accessories are available for ALL AGES AND SIZES, there is no judgement or labels here, just a comfortable and stress free environment for you to come and relax whilst making one of the biggest decisions of any occasion "Selecting Your Perfect Dress or Outfit".

Monday	CLOSED
Tuesday	CLOSED
Wednesday – Saturday	10am - 3pm
Sunday	CLOSED

Appointments can be booked out of these hours if more convenient.

DAVID THE JEWELLER
01305 773700

www.davidthejeweller.co.uk
sales@davidthejeweller.co.uk

At David the Jeweller we love what we do. We have a passion to fulfil our customers' requirements when celebrating life's most special occasions. Engagements, weddings, graduations and birthdays to name a few are usually marked with the purchase of a beautiful piece of jewellery or smart watch that may well become a valuable family heirloom.

This is why we use our expertise to bring you

Tell them Purdey sent you…

a range of distinctive fine quality jewellery in Platinum, Gold, Palladium or Silver and you can also choose from a stunning range of Diamonds and precious gemstones to be enjoyed for years to come.

In 1984 David Hughes took a job at a jeweller and quickly discovered what an interesting and rewarding profession the industry provides. With the ambition to open a shop of his own, he set about obtaining The National Association of Goldsmiths Retail Jewellers Diploma, then qualifying as a Fellow of the Gemmological Association of Great Britain and achieving the Diamond Grading Diploma. With over two decades of experience of fine jewellery and watches, in 2005 he opened the family-run shop in the beautiful Dorset seaside town of Weymouth (see picture) where you are most welcome to visit in person and experience the award-winning customer service for yourself.

We have a busy watch and jewellery repairs department staffed by skilled craftsmen as well as producing bespoke jewels to our customers specification. We also have a valuation service, for customers visiting in store.

We hope you enjoy shopping with us.

We are sure you will love what we do too.

Monday - Saturday   09:00 - 17:00
Sunday   CLOSED

Tell them Purdey sent you…

NAUTICO LOUNGE

01305 789242

www.facebook.com/nauticoloungeweymouth

https://thelounges.co.uk/nautico/

Nautico Lounge is an informal, neighbourhood food led cafe/bar open all-day everyday where families, friends, and locals can come for a drink or food. #vegan #dogfriendly

Signed, sealed and delivered! Nautico Lounge is in a really handsome old Post Office on St Thomas Street, right in the heart of Weymouth. Our lovely large and airy open plan space stretches back to great little garden out the back, so you should have no problem finding a spot to call your own. We serve a great range of food and drinks (including full kids, gluten free and vegan menus) in a really relaxed, welcoming atmosphere that includes buckets of old pictures and tremendously dangly tassel-y lightshades. Do look out for our beautiful mural behind the bar too, it's first class. Sorry.

Lounges was founded in 2002 by a trio of longstanding friends, Dave Reid, Alex Reilley and Jake Bishop. Having spent years in the restaurant and bar trade – not to mention just as many propping up the bars in Bristol (all of course in the name of research) – they decided

Tell them Purdey sent you…

it was time they did their own thing. The motivation was simple and very selfish; they wanted somewhere to drink themselves.

THE FLAMINGO ROOM
HAIR & BEAUTY
www.facebook.com/flamingohairbeauty/
hayleymooreflamingo@gmail.com
                                    01305 771297

NOUVEAU
TATTOO & AESTHETICS
  (No details found)

TESCO EXPRESS

COFFEE JAZZ   07435 592133
www.facebook.com/coffeejazzw/
coffee.jazz@outlook.com

   Est. August 2023. Weymouth's home for top-notch coffee, fresh fare and unbeatable service

Tell them Purdey sent you…

Tell them Purdey sent you…

STANLEYS
COFFEE SHOP

01305 839229

www.facebook.com/StanleysCoffeeShop/

Monday	CLOSED
Tuesday – Friday	09:00 - 17:30
Sunday	CLOSED

HARDY'S HOPHOUSE

01305 300324

www.hardyshophousepub.co.uk

    The pub's a place that's filled with all your faves. Family, friends, food, drink and laughs. We believe the food you enjoy and the drinks sip all help make your occasion extra special. That's why our menus are filled with the very

Tell them Purdey sent you…

best dishes for everyone to enjoy!

Why not try one of our show stopping burgers or tuck into pub classics, from fish and chips to hunters chicken. Don't forget to sip, say cheers or wash it all down with your favourite drinks. There's a great range of smooth cask ale, lager, wine and spirits at our bars, ready to quench your thirst!

So, head on down for satisfying food, drinks and a heartfelt welcome.

MAGPIE'S NEST 2 07403 598887

Monday, Tuesday, Thursday, Friday, Saturday	10:00 - 16:00
Wednesday	10:00 - 14:00
Sunday	CLOSED

STUART WILTSHIRE GLASS

01305 766037
0786 0541838

www.stuartwiltshireglass.co.uk
info@stuartwiltshireglass.co.uk

Stuart Wiltshire has been a glass artist for over 27 years now. His passion is creating unique hand-blown commissioned glass lighting chandeliers and distinctive features for interior and exterior commercial spaces and private residences.

His fresh and innovative approach to the art of glass blowing is overwhelming. He begins with meticulous planning in finding creative solutions to designing hot glass, not only paying attention to colour combinations, but also to the texture of the glass itself, then executing the project in the hot shop, creating the reality of the challenge presented by the client.

We currently enjoy making glass pieces with Cremation ashes as it seems to make people so happy, commissioning a piece of glass art with their loved one's ashes preserved inside, giving the piece much more meaning to them personally.

Stuart's glass hot shop and gallery can be found on the High Street, Weymouth a short stroll from the harbour bridge. There you will find a wide selection of art glass for sale in the form of bowls, vases, vessels, sculptures and

Tell them Purdey sent you…

handmade animals, plus you can walk in and commission Stuart Wiltshire Glass for beautiful unique hand casting impressions of your family members that will be available for collection or postage just 24 hours later.

WEYMOUTH EBIKE HIRE

01305 564563

www.weymouthebikehire.co.uk/

info@weymouthebikehire.co.uk

Born out of a love of cycling and the great outdoors, Weymouth Ebike hire was started in 2022 to provide high quality electric mountain bike rental and tours in Weymouth and the surrounding area. Here at Weymouth Ebike hire, we really do believe there is no better way to explore the beautiful Dorset coast than on an electric mountain bike, fast enough to cover some serious ground whilst taking in the sights this part of the country offers. Electric bikes make the countryside and cycling accessible to all ranges of fitness level, whether you want a leisurely amble or a more energetic day out, they can give you that little helping hand when the going gets tough. We are based in Weymouth, at the heart of the world-famous Jurassic coast. Whether you just need a electric mountain bike

Tell them Purdey sent you...

to create your own adventure or would like to participate in one of our guided tours we offer everything you want to make some amazing memories.

You will require proof of ID when collecting the bike e.g. passport, driving license or identity card. Unfortunately, due to UK law you must be at least 14 years of age to ride an eBike.
Each bike comes with helmet, lock and lights.

    Full Day   (0930-1630)   £50.00
    Half Day (3 hours)   £35.00
    Week   £275.00
    Additional full day   £40.00

Free delivery and collection for DT3 and DT4 postcodes. Please call to discuss delivery and collection to other areas.

Please call 01305 564563 to book your Ebike adventure. All our bikes get booked very quickly during busy periods so we recommend you book early to ensure we can reserve the correct size bike for your day out. We are very happy to discuss anything regarding your Ebike adventure and have a fantastic selection of routes available to make your ride a memorable experience.

Tell them Purdey sent you…

CAMBER CYCLE WORKS

01305 230319

www.cambercycleworks.com
www.facebook.com/cambercycleworks/

info@cambercycleworks.com

We are an independent rider-owned bicycle workshop, offering the full range of servicing and repairs, as well as restorations, wheel building, custom builds, frame repairs and modifications.

Monday - Friday   09:00 - 17:00
Saturday   10:00 - 16:00
Sunday   CLOSED

THE OUTLET

www.facebook.com/Theoutletweymouth/

We sell men's, women's & children's clothes. Popular brands for clearance prices!

Monday – Saturday   10:30 - 17:30
Sunday   CLOSED

COBBLEKEYS 'N' TEES

01305 568011

https://cobblekeys.co.uk/

Tell them Purdey sent you...

-a professional Shoe Repair Service; carried out by Dave who has in excess of 30 years experience.

-a precision Key Cutting Service which covers most cylinder and mortise keys, we also carry a range of pre-cut window keys

-a 3D Scan and Print service. This is a new service which we would like to expand so if you have any projects in mind please feel free to contact us to see what we can do.

-a while-you-wait Watch Battery changing service. We also carry and fit a range of watch straps; in addition to this we can replace spring bars and pins as well as re-sizing most bracelet straps.

-an Engraving service; we carry a range of engravable pet tags, hip flasks and tankards and also engrave plaques for trophies. Just ask us for further details

Printing

Mug Printing - We are able to print any picture or text onto a mug, whether it is a family snap or a child's drawing or a business logo. We can take pictures from most android phones via Bluetooth, or from email and even scan from hard copy.

Tee Shirts- We offer a vinyl print service and can print any text on our range of Fruit of the Loom tee shirts. If you would like to provide your own shirt we can print that too but please

Tell them Purdey sent you…

speak to us first to make sure the material and shirt design are printable.

Coasters- Like the mug printing, we can print almost anything on our metal coasters. These coasters are finished with cork stands on the underside to stop any scratches or hot marks on furniture.

We also print: Key fobs, Signs, Puzzles and compacts.

We are a local Weymouth business offering services to the public including, Shoe Repairs, Key Cutting, Engraving, Watch repairs/batteries/straps, T Shirt printing, sublimation, Dry Cleaning, Garment Repairs/Alterations, Lock fitting and always adding new services frequently including 3D printing (TBA).

We also sell a wide range of gifts including decorative wall plaques, metal ornaments, seaside gifts, patterned folding walking sticks and so much more…

Monday – Saturday   0900 – 1700
Sunday   10.30 – 1500

PLAYYARD   07582 415346

www.playyardweymouth.co.uk
www.facebook.com/PlayYardWeymouth/
Dorset's #magicalmixology cocktail bar
Home of the Mary Poppins Experiment, Dr

Tell them Purdey sent you...

Jones Antidote, Happy Chemical, Flamingogo, Strawberry Volcano ... & many more! Open every weekend!

Monday	18:00 - 00:00
Tuesday	CLOSED
Wednesday	18:00 - 00:00
Thursday	18:00 - 00:00
Friday	18:00 - 01:00
Saturday	15:00 - 02:00
Sunday	18:00 - 00:00

THE NAIL SHOP
(No details found)

SLUG & LETTUCE 01305 772913

www.slugandlettuce.co.uk/weymouth

At Slug and Lettuce Weymouth, every hour is happy hour – from weekday treats to Saturday night dancing, we're the perfect spot for hot deals, bites & cocktails to die for.

Let's get the good times flowing!

We are dog-friendly Sun-Fri

Saturdays are at manager's discretion - it may be too busy for furry friends!

Monday - Thursday:	12:00 - 11:00
Friday:	12:00 - 2:00
Saturday:	10:00 - 2:00
Sunday:	10:00 - 11:00

Tell them Purdey sent you…

JD WETHERSPOONS
THE SWAN
01305 750231

The 1864 map of Weymouth shows a brewery on part of the site now occupied by this Wetherspoon pub. The brewery later became The Swan Inn which stood here until the 1970s. The pub, which dates from Victorian times, seems to have been demolished around 1970.

J S KEBAB
01305 750810

www.jskebab.co.uk/

We have an exciting menu for you to explore, filled with loads of options for the whole family to enjoy. From traditional Turkish kebabs, to freshly made Pizzas, flamed grilled burger, plus delicious wraps, sides & much more. Here are some highlights.

Monday - Sunday   17:00 - 23:45

THE EDGE CAFÉ 07484 273030

edgerestaurantweymouth@gmail.com

www.facebook.com/edgecafeweymouth/

Independently owned serving home made cooked to order dishes that caters also for Vegetarian and Gluten Free. We are also dog

Tell them Purdey sent you…

friendly with disabled facilities.

Monday	CLOSED
Tuesday – Saturday	09:30 - 14:30
Sunday	CLOSED

CROWN HOTEL (No details found)

MARLBORO
FISH & CHIPS

01305 785700

www.marlbororestaurant.co.uk/
We are dog friendly in our takeaway but unfortunately not in our restaurant.

RENDEZVOUS   01305 761343

www.crafted-social.co.uk
www.crafted-social.co.uk/rendezvous-weymouth

Situated next door to Weymouth's picturesque harbour, our venue boasts three diverse floors and a gorgeous outdoor seating area, perfectly suited to any occasion, whether it be a cider in the sun, a relaxed family meal or even the party of the year, we've got you covered.

If you like all things Sporty, you'll LOVE our lower ground floor, The Anchor, a fully equipped 'man-cave-esque' Sports Bar with multiple HD screens showcasing live action all

Tell them Purdey sent you...

day. If that's not enough to keep you entertained, we've also got a pool table, electronic darts, fruit machines and a juke box as well as all of our great-value drinks deals and bar menu for refuelling!

Our cool & quirky main floor, Rendezvous, feels just like home away from home; enjoy friendly service and a great selection of delicious food from our full restaurant menus, colourful cocktails and real ales all within our fantastic family-friendly atmosphere. Rendezvous really is the premier choice for group meal or party bookings, catering for all ages and offering a wide range of eye-catching spaces that can be privately reserved! Why not try something a little different and book in for one of our exciting cocktail masterclasses where you can learn how to become a mixing pro?

Upstairs plays host to our luxuriously sleek nightclub, DAO, Weymouth's favourite party venue! Combine one of our top value drinks packages with a VIP booth for a prestige night of celebration or step-inside and join us to dance the night away with great music from one of our experienced in-house DJs; the best night out in town!

Tell them Purdey sent you…

NEW BOND STREET

POUNDLAND
NEW LOOK
JD SPORTS

WHITE HART   01305 785165
www.greeneking.co.uk/pubs/dorset/white-hart

The White Hart is a great local pub in the heart of the community, with friendly service and honest pricing. Fantastic menu and selection of drinks to suit all.

Monday – Saturday   11:00 - 11:00
Sunday   12:00 - 10:00
Serving hours
Monday – Sunday   12:00 - 9:00

ICELAND
THE RANGE
COSTA
PEACOCKS
SUPERDRUG

Tell them Purdey sent you…

ST MARY STREET

NAPOLI
GIFTS   01305 773731
Monday – Sunday   10 am–5 pm

BELLE'S
THE PINK CAKE SHOP

01305 782250

www.facebook.com/BellesTraditionalBakers
A traditional bakery with a bright pink twist!

Monday	CLOSED
Tuesday	CLOSED
Wednesday	CLOSED
Thursday	09:30 - 15:30
Friday	09:30 - 15:30
Saturday	09:00 - 16:00
Sunday	10:00 - 15:30

FOSSIL BEACH   01305 760817
107 St Mary Street   GIFT SHOP
www.fossilbeach.co.uk/
www.facebook.com/FossilBeachWeymouth

Tell them Purdey sent you…

Fossil beach is a bricks and mortar gift shop based in Weymouth Dorset at the heart of the Jurassic coast.

We sell a range of things of geological interest from Jurassic coast fossils to crystals and gemstones and mineral samples, Silver Celtic and pagan Jewellery, gemstone and semi-precious stone jewellery, metaphysical items, such as Runes sets, dowsers & wands, plus a massive range of semi-precious gemstone beads, charms, cords and chains alongside all the tools and findings you need to get creative making your own jewellery.

NATURAL INSPIRATIONS

01305 784514

www.facebook.com/NaturalInspirationsShop/

We stock a wide range of unusual and funky gifts, as well as beach/nautical decor to bring a little piece of the seaside into your life and home. All products are carefully chosen and are mainly ethically traded.

Monday - Saturday	10:00 - 17:30
Sunday	CLOSED

Tell them Purdey sent you…

GLADSTONES
JEWELLERS

01305 830423

https://gladstonesfamilyjewellers.co.uk/
www.facebook.com/GladstonesJewel/?rf=560753540752257

Gladstones is a traditional independent family run jewellers in the heart of Weymouth's vibrant town centre on the Jurassic Coast. We specialise in vintage and pre-owned jewellery and luxury watches. We're confident that you will always find something a bit different when you visit us.

We believe in traditional family values of honesty, integrity and trust and we pride ourselves in offering a warm and friendly welcome to our customers. Our small friendly team will be happy to go the extra mile to help you find exactly what you are looking for.

TATTOO MORNINGSTAR

01305 788884

www.facebook.com/tattoomorningstarweymouth/
https://tattoomorningstar.com/

With nearly 40 years of combined experience in tattooing, we pride ourselves on being one of the most diverse and skilled studios in Dorset.

Tell them Purdey sent you…

Situated a stone's throw away from Weymouth's infamous golden beach, our little studio was honoured to pick up England's Business Awards Best Studio in Dorset 2023.

Having opened our doors in 2019, our family run business is currently home to our 3 incredible resident artists and 2 highly skilled piercers.

From Traditional to Realism, fantasy to scenery, we have yet to find a challenge that cant be aced by one of our artists.

We can also do cover up work as well as tattoo removal and piercings as well.

We pride ourselves on having the friendliest and most relaxed atmosphere for you to be tattooed in as well as carry out the highest level of work for you!

Have a wonder around our website where you will meet the team and see some of our amazing work!

Please do give us a call if you have anything we may be able to help you with, or pop in and meet the team who will always be more than happy to help!

Monday	CLOSED
Tuesday – Saturday	10:00 – 17:00
Sunday	CLOSED

Tell them Purdey sent you…

CRUISE IN CAFÉ

www.cruiseincafe.co.uk
www.facebook.com/CruiseInCafeWeymouth/

Monday – Friday   9.30 – 3.00
Saturday   9.00 – 3.00
Sunday   10.00 – 2.00

SEATING OUTSIDE DOGFRIENDLY

SO SWEET

104 St Mary Street   SWEET SHOP
www.facebook.com/SoSweetShopUK/
www.sosweetshop.co.uk
NOT DOG FRIENDLY

The UK's Favourite Sweet Shop! 🍭
14 UK Stores, available online, app and TikTok Shop!

Monday - Sunday   09:00 - 18:00

NICETTA

St Mary Street   01305 839454
www.nicetta.co.uk/

www.facebook.com/Nicettarestaurant

Nicetta a love story of Pizza, pasta and all things Italian

Alvise and Dominique both came to the South West looking for new horizons. At Villa Nicetta, one of the most beautiful locations in

Tell them Purdey sent you...

Sicily, they got married.

With Dominique's roots in Weymouth they wanted to start a family business where their hearts lay.

After a lot of hard work, they transformed a tired property into a clean, comfortable, intimate restaurant. Alvise brought his Sicilian heritage, passion for great food and Dominique brought her long experience as a restaurant manager and together they have a fearless pursuit of high standards.

Today in Weymouth, you can taste a little piece of Sicily - Passion, flair and Family.

Sunday / Monday	CLOSED
Tuesday – Saturday	9am - 9pm
Food served from	11:30am - 8pm

FRITHS
OPTICIANS   01305 786303

weymouth@frithsopticians.co.uk
www.facebook.com/frithsopticiansweymouth

Our friendly independent Weymouth Practice

Monday - Friday	09:00 - 17:15
Saturday	09:00 - 17:00
Sunday	CLOSED

Tell them Purdey sent you…

THE BLACK DOG
01305   771426

The Black Dog Pub is the oldest pub in Weymouth.
blackdogweymouth@gmail.com
www.facebook.com/TheBlackDogWeymouth

MOVIL ZONE   01305 568082

www.facebook.com/MovilZoneLtd/
Repairs@movilzone.co.uk PHONE REPAIR

Monday – Friday	09:30 - 17:00
Saturday	10:00 - 17:00
Sunday	CLOSED

CLAIRE'S ACCESSORIES
01305 766885

https://stores.claires.com/gb-dor/weymouth/231.html

Monday – Saturday	9:00 - 5:30
Sunday	10:00 - 4:00

MARKS & SPENCER
01305 783881

Tell them Purdey sent you…

Monday - Saturday   08:30 - 18:00
Sunday   10:30 - 16:30

LITTLE DISHES   01305 319176

https://littledishesweymouth.com/
www.facebook.com/people/Little-Dishes-restaurant-bar/61552014077385/

Friday, Saturday,
Wednesday, Thursday   12:00 - 20:30
Sunday   12:00 - 16:00
Monday   CLOSED
Tuesday   CLOSED

BLUE CROSS CHARITY SHOP

COSTA   0845 600 8545

Monday – Sunday   0700 – 2000

DORSET BLIND ASSOCIATION
CHARITY SHOP

Monday – Saturday   10.00 – 5.00
Sunday   10.00 – 4.00

RIO'S PIRI PIRI   01305 770101

https://riospiripiriweymouth.co.uk/
www.facebook.com/RiosPiriPiriWeymouth/

Tell them Purdey sent you…

When they say their extra hot sauce is hot they really mean it!

Monday - Saturday   12:00 - 23:00
Sunday   14:00 - 23:00

BRITISH RED CROSS

CHARITY SHOP 🐺

NATIONWIDE

BONMARCHE   01305 774 983

www.bonmarche.co.uk/storelanding/?storename=Weymouth
www.facebook.com/BonmarcheWeymouth/

Monday – Saturday   9:00 - 5:30
Sunday   10:00 - 4:00

🐺

SCRIVENS HEARING CENTRE
                          01305 785 145

https://scrivens.com/branch/weymouth-2/

Monday - Saturday   9.00- 5.00
Sunday   CLOSED

Tell them Purdey sent you…

YOURS 01305 781611
www.yoursclothing.co.uk/
www.facebook.com/people/Yours-Clothing/100068115499347/

Monday - Saturday   09:00 - 17:30
Sunday   10:00 - 16:00

PHONE SPOT 07915 534581

www.facebook.com/phonespot93/
Monday - Saturday   09:00 - 18:00
Sunday   10:00 - 16:30

DEBRA
CHARITY SHOP   NOT DOG FRIENDLY

EVAPO 07399 734432
https://evapo.co.uk/vape-shops/weymouth
www.facebook.com/evapoweymouth
info@evapo.co.uk
Monday – Saturday
                         9:00 - 6:00
Sunday   10:00 - 4:00

Tell them Purdey sent you…

MOUNTAIN WAREHOUSE
01305 776076
www.mountainwarehouse.com/stores/wey/weymouth/

Monday - Saturday   09:00 - 18:00
Sunday   10:00 - 16:00

MADE IN ITALY
www.made-in-italy.com/

BOOTS OPTICIANS
01305 750936
www.boots.com
Monday - Saturday   09:00 - 17:30
Sunday   CLOSED

O2

HSBC

Tell them Purdey sent you…

THE WORKS   01305 770545
BOOKS & STATIONERY
www.facebook.com/TheWorksWeymouth

www.theworks.co.uk/

Always useful and it is amazing what books, toys and stationery, craftwork and other useful things they have. You can buy in store or order on line and pick up your package later.

Monday – Saturday   09:00 - 17:30
Sunday   10:00 - 16:00

PANDORA   01305 789476,
                 01305 782323
19 St Mary Street   JEWELLERY

HALIFAX

WEIRD FISH   01305 782800
www.weirdfish.co.uk/help/find-a-store/weymouth-store
www.facebook.com/people/Weird-Fish-Clothing/100089920459085/

Tell them Purdey sent you…

Based on St Mary Street, our Weymouth store has gone from strength to strength. With our clothing having a relaxed and laid back feel, we are a perfect fit in this lovely seaside town with locals and holiday makers alike.

Monday - Saturday	09:30 - 5:00
Sunday	10:00 - 4:00

GREGGS 01305 782352

www.greggs.co.uk/

Monday - Saturday	07:00 - 19:00
Sunday	07:30 - 17:00

NOT DOG FRIENDLY

VISION EXPRESS 01305 839071

Monday - Saturday	09:00 - 17:30
Sunday	CLOSED

THE WEYMOUTH SWEET SHOP

John Bull Confectioners 01305 750197

www.facebook.com/pages/The-Weymouth-Sweet-Shop/166031240123511
https://john-bull.com/

Monday - Saturday	09:00 - 17:30
Sunday	10:00 - 16:00

Tell them Purdey sent you...

FONE WORLD   01305 750577

www.facebook.com/foneworldweymouth25/

weymouth@foneworlduk.com

Fone world offer new sales, used sales, and repairs for mobile phones and electrical devices.

Monday - Saturday   09:00 - 18:00
Sunday   10:00 - 17:00

CORNISH BAKEHOUSE
                              01305 759765

www.cornish-bakehouse.com
www.just-eat.co.uk/restaurants-cornish-bakehouse-weymouth/menu

We are dedicated to hand-crafting some of Cornwall's best pasties. All our Pasties are hand-crimped in the traditional way and filled with only the finest quality ingredients. We use amazingly fresh beef from local suppliers when possible and from quality, farm-assured breeders from around the British Isles. Our pasties are then baked to perfection in our shops, fresh throughout the day. The result is a delicious, hearty pasty that is sure to satisfy.

Monday - Saturday   08:30 - 17:30
Sunday   10:00 - 16:00

Tell them Purdey sent you…

VODAFONE 0333 304 0191
Monday - Saturday 09:00 - 17:30
Sunday 10:00 - 16:00

THREE 01305 782972
Monday - Saturday 09:00 - 17:30
Sunday 10:30 - 16:30

SELL & REPAIR 01305 777554
www.facebook.com/people/Sellrepair-weymouth/100032389404320/

Sell your unwanted devices, repairs of laptops and phone , cases , portable chargers, earphones.
Monday - Saturday 09:00 - 17:30
Sunday CLOSED

Tell them Purdey sent you…

F HINDS 01305 782637
www.fhinds.co.uk/store-details?name=Weymouth
Monday - Saturday   09:00 - 17:30
    Sunday   CLOSED

CANCER RESEARCH UK
CHARITY SHOP
  www.cancerresearchuk.org   01305 780635

Monday - Saturday   09:00 - 17:30
Sunday   10:00 - 16:00

PHONE STUDIO
Monday - Saturday   09:00 - 17:30
Sunday   CLOSED

CARD FACTORY 01305 789392
www.cardfactory.co.uk/
Monday - Saturday   09:00 - 17:30
Sunday   10:30 - 16:30
NOT DOG FRIENDLY

134

Tell them Purdey sent you…

EE
01305 765690

Monday - Saturday	09:00 - 17:30
Sunday	10:30 - 16:30

KFC
01305 772701

Monday - Sunday 11:00 - 21:00

GIGI'S CAFÉ
01305 602159

www.facebook.com/Gigiscaffe/

gigiscoffeeshop@gmail.com

Recently open in central Weymouth, we have lovingly renovated to a high standard. Our ethos is to provide top quality produce in a very relaxed atmosphere.

To achieve the combination of excellence and sustainability we are using a top brand ECO Coffee

Monday - Saturday	08:00 - 21:00
Sunday	10:00 - 16:00

SALTROCK
01305 759720

www.saltrock.com/

Monday - Saturday 09:00 - 17:30

Tell them Purdey sent you…

Sunday   10:30 - 16:30

HOLLAND & BARRETT
www.hollandandbarrett.com/stores/weymouth-3454/

   Our stores cannot be reached by telephone. Our Customer Service team is available for calls on 0330 058 2640. Bank holiday hours may vary.

Monday – Saturday   09:00 - 17:00
Sunday   10:30 - 16:30
NOT DOG FRIENDLY

SHOEZONE   01305 761491
www.shoezone.com
Monday – Saturday   09:00 - 17:30
Sunday   10:00 - 16:00

BRITISH HEART FOUNDATION
                                01305 785457
www.facebook.com/BHFWeymouth/
                                CHARITY SHOP

Monday – Saturday   09:30 - 17:00
Sunday   11:00 - 17:00

Tell them Purdey sent you...

COFFEE #1   01305 783192
www.coffee1.co.uk

Opening our doors in 2001 and inspired by the prospect of giving customers a more complete experience, Coffee#1 has remained true to the values we established on day one and that's to make it locally loved - serving great coffee made by talented baristas, in a relaxed and welcoming environment where your time is your own.

If you're looking for somewhere to recharge yourself after a bit of shopping or need to grab a coffee before heading to the beach, Coffee#1 Weymouth is a great stop. A beautiful old building, inside you'll find some cosy corners where you can hide away and unwind. Or pick up a great title from our bookcase and while away the hours.

Monday - Saturday   07:30 - 17:30
Sunday   09:00 - 17:00

LIMELIGHT   01305 781888
CLOTHING

https://limelightboutique.co.uk/
www.facebook.com/limelight

boutiquelimelight@gmail.com

Tell them Purdey sent you…

Limelight Boutique has been a firm favourite for women locally in Dorset for over 20 years. Situated in the heart of Weymouth, Limelight continues to serve it's customers online too!

Monday – Saturday   09:30 - 17:00
Sunday   CLOSED
Haven Owners Discount 10%

KOOKY BLOOM

www.kookybloom.com

Hair Accessories & Gifts.   Real Flower Jewellery.

Hi from us! My name is Sophie and I am the very proud outnumbered Mum in a house of boys! (Husband and two children Max & Teddy) and we are based in Dorset on the quirky Isle of Portland.

Kooky Bloom begun simply through my love of everything floral, unusual and fashion! My overall goal was to combine them all to create the most gorgeous & Unique items for the world to see. I really enjoy being able to create items that are beautiful yet meaningful to each individual person.

Although I am the creator of the items, my Husband Matt is the "Admin team" and our boys are our inspiration. It's the dream to be doing something I am so passionate but all

Tell them Purdey sent you...

the while maintaining a good work/life balance with our family.
We hope you enjoy & love our creations as much we do making them!
Hi from us! My name is Sophie and I am the very proud outnumbered Mum in a house of boys! (Husband and two children Max & Teddy) and we are based in Dorset on the quirky Isle of Portland.
Kooky Bloom begun simply through my love of everything floral, unusual and fashion! My overall goal was to combine them all to create the most gorgeous & Unique items for the world to see. I really enjoy being able to create items that are beautiful yet meaningful to each individual person.
Although I am the creator of the items, my Husband Matt is the "Admin team" and our boys are our inspiration. It's the dream to be doing something I am so passionate but all the while maintaining a good work/life balance with our family.
We hope you enjoy & love our creations as much we do making them!

Tell them Purdey sent you…

Monday – Saturday	10.00 – 17.00
Sunday	11.00 – 15.00

NHS DISCOUNT 10%

CeX 0330 123 5986

www.facebook.com/CeXWeymouth/

Monday - Saturday	09:00 - 18:00
Sunday	10:00 - 17:00

Tell them Purdey sent you…

PEACHES   07990 571928

Woman's clothing shop based in Weymouth, Sherborne & New Milton

www.facebook.com/people/Peaches-Italy/100067362916868/

FANTASTIC SAUSAGE
01305 766212

https://thefantasticsausagefactory.co.uk/our-sausages/
www.thefantasticsausagefactory.co.uk

Here at The Fantastic Sausage Factory, we are a family run butchers, headed by Dennis Spurr, with over 40 years of experience in the trade and at one time ran the biggest butcher's shop in the country We are a traditional, well respected family run Butchers established in 1992 in Weymouth and are dedicated to producing and serving a variety of delicious, quality, Artisan Sausages, skilfully produced to our own special recipes for great flavour and texture We're Crazy for Super Sausages Some recipes date back over 100 years and to ensure a top quality sausage, we only source the highest quality meats and other top quality ingredients.

Tell them Purdey sent you…

TAKE AWAY FOOD (With tables outside)
Monday - Saturday   09:00 - 17:30
Sunday   CLOSED

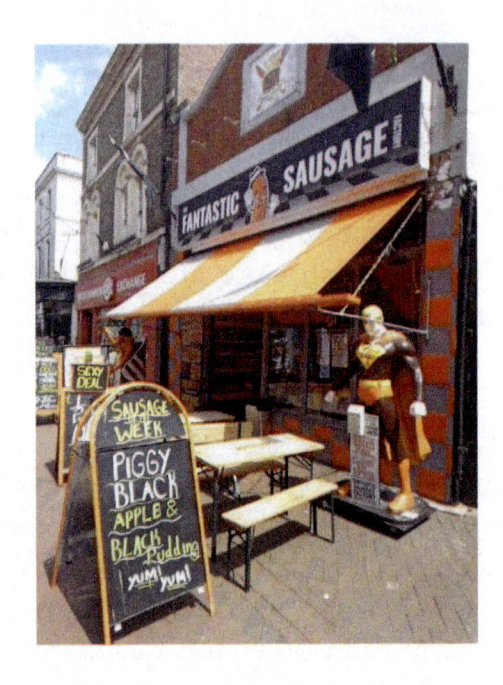

Tell them Purdey sent you…

JULIA'S HOUSE   01305 785072
CHARITY SHOP

Monday - Saturday	09:00 - 17:00
Sunday	CLOSED
Summer	10.00 – 16.00

BREEZE
SKIN & BEAUTY   01305 769996
www.facebook.com/BreezeTheSalonWeymouth/
breezethesalon@gmail.com

We are a much loved local Beauty Clinic who provide a wide range of Beauty Treatments since 2012.

Monday	09:00 - 15:00
Tuesday	09:30 - 17:30
Wednesday	09:30 - 17:30
Thursday	09:30 - 20:00
Friday	09:30 - 17:30
Saturday	09:00 - 15:00
Sunday	10:00 - 15:00

Tell them Purdey sent you…

THE BAG SHOP   01305 778783
https://thebagshopltd.co.uk/

We are specialist independent retailers with an ethos to provide a large selection of diverse and quality products at competitive prices while offering informative and helpful customer service.

Our range at The Bag Shop includes: handbags, holdalls, rucksacks, purses, wallets, luggage and associated products The Bag Shop family currently includes two standalone shops on the South Coast of England and a dedicated online store.

We are a family run business which has been involved in the retail of bags and luggage since the early 90's Originally starting trading on open air markets, the concept of a specialist discount bag shop evolved and soon afterwards several stores were opened.

Currently there are still two standalone retail Bag Shops trading on the South Coast of England, one in Weymouth and one in Boscombe (a suburb of Bournemouth). We are passionate about trying to retain physical stores in the high street where customers can still come and look and touch the products first hand, but also appreciate the retail sector is

Tell them Purdey sent you…

changing massively, so now have created a dedicated online store where customers can now get that virtual experience.

We sincerely hope you enjoy your visit to The Bag Shop whether online or in store.

Monday - Saturday   09:00 - 17:30
Sunday   10:00 - 16:00

CORNUCOPIA
ANTIQUES CRAFTS AND COLLECTABLES   07711 791579

www.facebook.com/people/Cornucopia-Antiques-Crafts-and-Collectables/100064168687351/

theoldrectory12@live.co.uk

Monday – Saturday   10:00 - 15:00
Sunday   CLOSED

WESSEX PHOTO   01305 782329

https://wessexphoto.com/
www.facebook.com/wessexphoto/

weymouth@wessexphoto.com

Monday – Saturday   09:00 - 17:00
Sunday   CLOSED

Tell them Purdey sent you…

WEYMOUTH MOBILITY
01305 760575

www.weymouthmobilityltd.co.uk
www.facebook.com/people/Weymouth-Mobility/100063483281366/

Welcome to Weymouth Mobility. We're an independent, family-owned supplier of high-quality rise and recline chairs, mobility scooters and electric beds. Based in Weymouth, we offer a wide range of expertly made products throughout Dorset. For quality mobility products and daily living aids, contact Weymouth Mobility Ltd to find out more about our range of products. We provide solutions for both sale and hire, so that you have a range of options to match your needs.

| Monday - Saturday | 09:00 - 17:00 |
| Sunday | CLOSED |

ARTISAN ISLAND 07401 008004

www.facebook.com/artisanislandweymouth/
https://artisanisland.co.uk/

We have over 200 individual sellers, if you visit Weymouth area you most definitely want to call in and see us, there are some amazing items

Tell them Purdey sent you…

made by some very talented people.

Artisan Island is a place for hand-made crafts, high end collectables and anything else that fits within those realms.

Monday – Saturday   10:00 – 5:00
Sunday   ?

TRESPASS 01305 778304

Monday - Saturday   09:00 - 17:30
Sunday   10:30 - 16:30

TIDAL VAPE 01305 233450

https://tidalvape.co.uk/
www.facebook.com/people/Tidal-Vape/100095122192690/

Monday - Saturday   08:30 - 18:00
Sunday   09:00 - 17:00

PURE
HAIR & BEAUTY   01305 561789

www.facebook.com/Purehairandbeautyweymouth/
Friday   09:00 - 17:30
Saturday   09:00 - 16:30
Sunday   CLOSED

Tell them Purdey sent you…

MUSTARD SEEDS GALLERY
Dog Friendly Arts & Crafts St Mary's Church
Handmade Local Crafts Fundraising for Church
Volunteer run to sell for local people

Monday – Saturday   10.30 – 3.30
Sunday   CLOSED

LA LUNA
GIFTS   01305 766936
www.facebook.com/lalunaweymouth/
Laluna45@btinternet.com

La Luna in St Mary St has been a must visit independent store for gifts, clothing and accessories for over twenty years. They also stock a nice range of greetings cards.

Monday - Saturday   09:00 - 17:30
Sunday   CLOSED

HEART DECO
GIFTS & INTERIORS
56a St Mary Street GIFT SHOP 07891 846003
https://heartdeco.co.uk/
www.facebook.com/heartdecoweymouth/

Tell them Purdey sent you…

hello@heartdeco.co.uk

Established 2011

Heart Deco started as a family run bricks and mortar gift and interiors store in 2011 in the coastal resort of Weymouth in Dorset. Following its success and responding to the demand from our many lovely visitors we opened our new on-line store in 2019. We work hard sourcing products to offer you a unique range of handpicked gifts and home accessories that we hope will make your home a joyful and relaxing space. Our eclectic range of products also make for wonderful thoughtful gifts that are a delight to give but that you will also want to keep yourself!

Gifts: We want you to love the gift that you give whether to others or as a present to yourself.

If you love indoor plants and flowers and are either starting out with a collection or already have a few plants at home we always have a wide selection of unusual plant pots and vases in stock to help you arrange them in a more stylish and creative way.

Fragrance and candlelight also has an important effect on mood and ambience and we have a range of aromatherapy candles and room diffusers specially selected to either soothe or energise your space all made with natural oils and plant waxes so no nasties in there to pollute your home. To compliment these products, we also have a range of books which have been hand selected to encourage well-being and boost happiness.

Interiors: We are passionate about interiors and always have something new and exciting in our upstairs showroom.

Inspired by our location we always have a range of home accessories which help to inject a relaxed coastal charm into your space. This includes products using natural materials such as seagrass hanging baskets, willow and bamboo lanterns and driftwood hearts and decor.

HALLS KITCHEN 01305 839839
www.facebook.com/hallskitchen2019/
jason@hallskitchen.co.uk

Halls Kitchen is a premier and authentic Restaurant that has been proudly serving the Weymouth area and beyond since 2018.

Since then, our mission has been to provide high-quality food for all those that wish to combine fun and enjoyable ambiance with skilful cooking into one extraordinary dining experience.

This cozy establishment highlights our passion for market-fresh ingredients, honest

Tell them Purdey sent you...

cooking, and an enjoyable atmosphere. Our menu features a selection of dishes, all made in-house by our talented chef.

With some of the most delicious combinations of ingredients, there is something for everyone to enjoy. Loved by locals and traveling foodies alike, now is the perfect time for you to join us today at Halls Kitchen.

Lunch
Friday – Saturday:	12 – 2:30
Sunday:	CLOSED

Dinner
Monday:	CLOSED
Tuesday – Saturday:	6pm – 10:30
Sunday:	CLOSED

MONA'S
THAI AND ASIAN   01305 787265

www.facebook.com/monasthaicuisine/

Saturday	12:00 - 14:00
	17:30 - 21:30
Sunday	CLOSED
Monday	CLOSED
Tuesday	17:30 - 21:30
Wednesday	17:30 - 21:30
Thursday	12:00 - 14:00
	17:30 - 21:30
Friday	12:00 - 14:00
	17:30 - 21:30

Tell them Purdey sent you…

UPSTAIRS DOWNSTAIRS

01305 781000

www.facebook.com/UpstairsDownWey/

"Simple Food Cooked Well"

Small established cafe in the heart of Weymouth since 1988

Monday - Sunday   07:00 - 15:00

THE GOLDEN LION

PUB   01305 788802

www.facebook.com/goldenlionwey/

PAZ CLOTHING   01305 777693

Saturday   09:45 - 17:30
Sunday   11:00 - 15:00
Monday - Friday   10:30 - 16:30

BABS & PITTA (No details available)

Tell them Purdey sent you…

ST EDMUND STREET

WEYMOUTH ANGLING CENTRE LTD

2 St Edmund Street   FISHING   01305 777771
https://weymouthangling.com/

Weymouth Angling Centre was opened in 1996 by Andy and Charlotte Selby. Over the last 20 years the business has built a reputation of offering an extensive range of sea angling products, alongside trusted advice and knowledge from friendly local staff. Andy and the team select a range of popular and specialist products from the leading industry brands and endeavour to cater to anglers from sea, coarse and carp disciplines. Approachable and skilled staff are familiar with all aspects of fishing and will give unbiased information on any product and share local fishing knowledge. Known locally as WAC (Weymouth Angling Centre) the Centre values its loyal customers and continues to welcome new customers to the shop and online store every day.

The shop is seconds from the beautiful Weymouth harbour on the Jurassic coast, open seven days a week, The online store offers 24

Tell them Purdey sent you…

hour shopping, a guide to fishing locally in the surrounding area and supports the local charter boat fleet.

Monday - Saturday   06:30 - 17:00
Sunday   06:30 - 16:00

FOX AESTHETICS
www.facebook.com/foxaestheticss/
www.foxaestheticss.com/

- A&E Nurse.
- Advanced aesthetics trained
- Alumier skincare stockist
- Booking link on website

I have been a qualified adult A&E Nurse for the last 8 years and have combined my passion for nursing with my love of beauty and trained in aesthetics.

All of my training has been completed with award winning, leading training providers. I am advanced aesthetics trained and have completed a wide variety of courses so that I can offer you the latest treatments, looks & techniques.

With my medical background and training in aesthetics complications you can be assured you're in safe hands.

Monday   CLOSED
Tuesday   10:00 - 18:00
Wednesday   09:00 - 17:00
Thursday   12:00 - 20:00

Tell them Purdey sent you...

Friday	09:00 - 13:00
Saturday	09:00 - 12:00
Sunday	CLOSED

MAGPIE'S NEST   07403 598887

Saturday	10:00 - 16:00
Sunday	CLOSED
Monday	10:00 - 16:00
Tuesday	10:00 - 16:00
Wednesday	10:00 - 14:00
Thursday	10:00 - 16:00
Friday	10:00 - 16:00

LONDIS

NAPOLI
PIZZA   01305 781706

www.pizzanapoli.co.uk/
www.facebook.com/NapoliWemouth/

You can watch our chefs tossing the dough

This impressive display is not just for your entertainment, there's more to it.

Tossing the dough helps retain the correct amount of moisture. Air flow over the doughs surface dries it out just enough to make it easier to handle and this technique makes for a perfect

Tell them Purdey sent you...

crispy crust so we can create a perfect pizza for you.

It is very important to us to buy the freshest ingredients but also to buy Italian produce and we are very lucky to have found a wonderful family run Italian supplier.

Our gosney oven is certainly something we love.

We spent time sourcing her locally, she is made of stone and gas fired reaching a perfect temperature of around 370 degrees which means you only have to wait about 4 minutes for your pizza to cook.

Saturday	16:00 - 00:00
Sunday	16:00 - 22:00
Monday - Friday	17:00 - 22:00

THE OLD HARBOUR
FISH & CHIPS

01305 458772

https://theoldharbourfishandchips.co.uk/
www.facebook.com/people/The-old-harbour-fish-and-chips/100057438490646/

Sunday - Thursday	11:30 - 10:00
Friday	11:30 - 10:30
Saturday	11:30 - 10:30

Tell them Purdey sent you…

MAIDEN STREET

Look out for the cannon ball in the wall…

THE DOGGY SHOP

07976 970969

www.thedoggieshop.co.uk/   Cash Only

Helping to keep you and your best friends safe.

Good selection of veterinary products, foods, treats, toys, leads, harnesses and all pet products.

Personal old-fashioned service

An amazingly well stocked shop with a lovely selection of good quality snacks, dog food and leads etc. Friendly staff, lovely shop and definitely worth your while to help out in these difficult times. A great reason to shop locally.

Saturday	09:30 - 15:00
Sunday	CLOSED
Monday	09:30 - 16:00
Tuesday	09:30 - 16:00
Wednesday	CLOSED
Thursday	09:30 - 16:00
Friday	09:30 - 16:00

Tell them Purdey sent you…

THE GREEDY SEAGULL
RESTAURANT
Mediterranean Restaurant
Maiden Street   07375 927829
www.facebook.com/thegreedyseagullrestaurant
We are dog friendly. Just let us know when you book, and we will arrange the room table for your dog.

FISH N FRITZ   01305 766386
9 Market Street
www.fishnfritz.co.uk
   Temporarily closed due to a fire.

THE MARKET HOUSE
                            01305 771236
www.facebook.com/markethousetavern/
   Local Traditional Pub just a short walk from Weymouth Harbour. Home to the Weymouth Cider Company Serving Real Ales (4) and Traditional Ciders (17) Sky Sports, BT Sports & Amazon.

   Saturday   12:00 - 23:00
   Sunday - Friday   12:00 - 00:00

AON
THAI KITCHEN   07362 439185
www.facebook.com/people/Aon-Thai-

Tell them Purdey sent you…

Kitchen-Weymouth/61552771302785/
Aonthaikitchen@gmail.com

Monday	CLOSED
Tuesday - Saturday	12:00 - 15:00
	17:00 - 21:00
Sunday	CLOSED

BOND STREET

RUDE NOT TO   01305 785770

12 Bond Street   CLOTHING & RETRO

www.rudenotto.net
www.facebook.com/pages/Rude-Not-To/154565234571415

rude-not-to@hotmail.co.uk

Established in 1956, rude not to… is the UK's original alternative clothing retailer and has been selling men's and women's, fashion. Fuelled by a love of Ska, 2 Tone, Northern Soul, Mod and R&B music we've been at the front line of the alternative clothing scene for more than 60 years bringing you the best designs in fashion. Rude not to… stocks whatever you want, Skinhead, Mod, Ska, 2 Tone, clothes, footwear and accessories first along with the coolest Suits, Original Harringtons, T-Shirts, and shoes from the

Tell them Purdey sent you…

world's hottest UK brands.

Saturday	09:00 - 17:00
Sunday	CLOSED
Monday	09:00 - 17:00
Tuesday	09:00 - 17:00
Wednesday	CLOSED
Thursday	09:00 - 17:00
Friday	09:00 - 17:00

ACUTT'S 01305 782656

www.facebook.com/profile.php?id=100057072535422

Acutt's is a Family run business, it has been in Weymouth for over 100 years. We supply Men's Work wear, Outsize Clothing and footwear

Saturday	09:00 - 13:00
	14:00 - 17:00
Sunday	CLOSED
Monday	09:00 - 13:00
	14:00 - 17:00
Tuesday	09:00 - 13:00
	14:00 - 17:00
Wednesday	09:00 - 13:00
	14:00 - 17:00
Thursday	09:00 - 13:00
	14:00 - 17:00
Friday	09:00 - 17:00

Tell them Purdey sent you…

PHIL'S VINYL VAULT
01305 786969

https://philsvinylvault.co.uk/
www.facebook.com/philsvinylvault/

Independent record store specialising in collectible LP records. Limited stock of singles (45's) and CD's. Music merchandise also available; mugs, t shirts, turntable slipmats etc.

Established in 2015 when I started with a couple of boxes of records, gradually building to where I am today with a shop full of quality second hand vinyl records. I also sell a limited amount of new vinyl, but my passion is original, collectable vinyl.

We are THE place to buy and sell records

Band Merchandise

Posters

Vinyl related tote bags

An exciting range of tankards, shot glasses, goblets

Records

Gift vouchers

Gig tickets on sale for select events at Weymouth Pavilion

Monday - Saturday   09:30 - 17:00
Sunday   CLOSED

Tell them Purdey sent you…

NEW STREET

WIGGLE BUBBLE TEA
01305 788806

www.facebook.com/W2shakies/
373784118@qq.com

Monday - Saturday   11:00 - 19:00
Sunday   11:00 - 18:00

1 STOP BEACH & GIFT SHACK
07835 450313

Bigger than it looks from the outside and has a downstairs. Beach Goods, Gifts, Home Made Jewellery and Mr Whippy!

ST ALBAN STREET

KING OF HEARTS 07961 033077

www.facebook.com/people/King-of-Hearts-Weymouth/100082828917457/

Our sister shop to Queen of Hearts Weymouth at 10 St Alban Street.

Tell them Purdey sent you…

Beach side gift shop selling inflatables, gifts, ice creams and lots more.

THE CRUSTY COB 01305 784605

www.facebook.com/Dorsetcake/posts/3578996872187098/

Saturday	08:30 - 15:45
Sunday	CLOSED
Monday - Friday	08:30 - 16:00

DRINK INC   07508 588949

www.facebook.com/Drinkincweymouth/

Monday - Saturday	11:00 - 16:30
Sunday	11:00 - 16:00

BAAN 57   01305 594739

www.facebook.com/Baan57/
info@baan57.co.uk
www.baan57.co.uk/

Crystals, Gemstones, Incense and Holders, Essential Oils, Metaphysical, Buddhas, Tarot and Oracle Cards, Salt Lamps, Soaps and Candles, Fantasy and Gothic, Hemp and Boho Bags.

Tell them Purdey sent you...

Called Baan 57 to continue the name from their previous shop. Baan means House in Thai and it was at number 57. They had such a following that they wanted to keep the name going.

Monday - Sunday   09:00 - 17:00

RAZMATAZZ   01305 783522
Geek Merchandise
www.razmatazz.co.uk/
www.facebook.com/razmatazzGifts/
shop@razmatazz.co.uk
NOT DOG FRIENDLY
Monday – Saturday   1000 – 1700
Sunday   1100 – 1600

SUTTONS
COFFEE SHOP   01305 786168
www.facebook.com/profile.php?id=100063605588753

Dogs are not permitted inside the coffee shop, but we do have 2 tables of 4 outside (and fresh water for our 4-legged friends).

Saturday   08:00 - 16:30
Sunday   CLOSED
Monday - Friday   08:00 - 16:00

Tell them Purdey sent you…

BIJA

01305 568832

www.facebook.com/people/Bija/100063381360233/
sales@bijaonline.co.uk
https://bijaonline.co.uk/

Bija Weymouth and Bija-Online offer a range of clothing, home furnishings, unique and spiritual gifts from around the world.

Our buying team visit each of our suppliers in person, both overseas and in the UK. It's a tough job but someone's gotta do it.

This helps to ensure we trade fairly and ethically, supporting local communities and building long-lasting relationships. It also means we bring you gorgeous products at the very best price.

Monday – Sunday   10.00 – 17.00

Tell them Purdey sent you…

ROLY'S FUDGE   07793 011206

www.facebook.com/RolysFudgeWeymouth/
weymouth@rolysfudge.co.uk
https://rolysfudge.co.uk/

Roly's Fudge Weymouth is a handmade fudge pantry specialising in the very best of traditional, crumbly fudge.

Originating from Devon in the West Country over 35 years ago, we now have independently-run family fudge pantries across the UK. Each artisan shop uses traditional recipes to make fresh fudge every day, handmade in full view for you to see.

Roly's Fudge started in 1987 when the founders started to make homemade fudge in their farmhouse cottage kitchen. They decided to return to the artisan method of making fudge – no oils or additives were needed, just finest quality ingredients made with only traditional methods.

Using a large copper cauldron obtained from a Devon antique shop, they followed an old family recipe passed down over generations to make the first batch of traditional vanilla clotted cream, using lashings of Devon butter.

No artificial colourings or flavourings, emulsifiers, additives or palm oils… ever!

Monday -Friday   09:30 - 18:00
Saturday - Sunday   10:00 - 18:00

Tell them Purdey sent you…

MY LITTLE HAT SHOP
www.mylittlehatshop.co.uk
Hats, Socks, Summer Clothing

Monday – Sunday   10.00 – 17.00

BIBI'S BOUTIQUE & BIBIs HOME
01305 788488

www.bibisboutique.co.uk/
www.facebook.com/bibisboutiquedorset/

An independent, quirky boutique stocking unique and individual clothes, accessories and gifts.

Saturday   09:30 - 17:30
Sunday   11:00 - 16:00
Monday   10:00 - 17:00

THE RETRO CLOSET
www.facebook.com/rosiesretroclosett/
https://rosiesretrocloset.wixsite.com/rosiesretrocloset
rosiesretrocloset@gmail.com

Rosie's Retro Closet opened its doors in April of 2022 to0 help our small town with

Tell them Purdey sent you…

shopping sustainably. When we moved into our current store it was important we incorporated other small, sustainable local businesses to share the love of conscious purchasing. From clothing to homeware accessories, there's something for everyone in our quirky shop!

Monday	CLOSED
Tuesday - Saturday :	10:30 - 5:00
Sunday:	CLOSED

MUFFINS COFFEE HOUSE

01305 783844

www.facebook.com/muffinsstalbans/
muffinscoffeehouseweymouth@gmail.com

Family run Café providing exceptional breakfasts and afternoon teas cooked by Geoff, Chef/Proprietor.

Monday - Saturday	09:00 - 16:30
Sunday	09:00 - 16:00

NOT DOG FRIENDLY

QUEEN OF HEARTS

01305 773336

www.facebook.com/queenofheartsweymouth/
queenofheartsweymouth@outlook.com

Monday - Saturday	09:30 - 17:30
Sunday	10:30 - 15:00

Tell them Purdey sent you…

ST ALBAN STREET GALLERY & WEYMOUTH WOOLEYS

07702 072804

www.facebook.com/people/St-Alban-Street-Gallery/100048446812763/

This Gallery combines locally made and inspired products with a lovely wool and yarn shop. Arts and crafts and wool. Items from Local Artists & Craftworkers.

Saturday	10:00 - 16:00
Sunday	11:00 - 16:00
Monday	10:00 - 16:00
Tuesday	09:00 - 16:00
Wednesday	11:00 - 16:00
Thursday	10:00 - 16:00
Friday	10:00 - 16:00

EAST STREET

CUTTER HOTEL

01305 761845

www.cutterhotelweymouth.co.uk
www.facebook.com/people/Cutter-Hotel-

Dogs Welcome. Food from Shop next door can be eaten in Lounge Bar

Tell them Purdey sent you…

Weymouth/100089629105333/

Cutter Hotel is a 4 bedroom hotel with an integral Bar/Pub which holds weekly fun & music events.

Monday - Thursday	12:00 - 23:00
Friday	12:00 - 00:00
Saturday	11:00 - 00:00
Sunday	11:00 - 23:00

THE OLDEN NEW 07711 294340

www.facebook.com/rebecor2020/
theoldennew.email@gmail.com

》 South West furniture artist
》 Vintage & New Homewares
》 Commissions Welcome

FOR SALE, Couldn't see if it was open or not.

Tell them Purdey sent you...

ESPLANADE

ALEXANDRA GARDENS
01305 784970
www.facebook.com/people/Alexandra-Gardens-Weymouth/100057827642586/
AMUSEMENT ARCADE
www.facebook.com/people/Alexandra-Gardens-Arcade-Family-Amusement-Park/100095610697785/

Monday – Thursday	12:00 - 23:00
Friday	12:00 - 00:00
Saturday	11:00 - 00:00

THE CACTUS TEA ROOMS
01305 778934

www.facebook.com/cactustearooms/
cactustearooms@gmail.com

Tea Room, Cafe, Bistro and Bar, situated by the beach in sunny Weymouth

Saturday	CLOSED
Sunday	CLOSED
Monday – Friday	09:30 - 17:00

Tell them Purdey sent you…

THE WHITE PEPPER

01305 750694

www.facebook.com/thewhitepepperweymouth
thewhitepepper@outlook.com
https://thewhitepepper.co.uk/

Tea Room, Cafe, Bistro and Bar, situated by the beach in sunny Weymouth.

The White pepper is the home of Kerala cuisine, which has evolved over centuries to perfection, that will leave you wanting more. Each Keralan dish is prepared with a variety of spices used in the Keralan cuisine that is well known.

CHEF PATRON LOUIS

Chef Louis has worked in various restaurants in the past 20 years, in many countries across the globe. Now, Louis and his family have made their home in the western country.

Louis aims to bring authentic Keralan flavours to the southwest coast of England. These flavours have never been experienced in this region before.

Chef Louis first started the white pepper at his home kitchen in Yeovil. Now he has an opportunity to open a restaurant takeaway in Weymouth, Dorset. His concept is to provide an authentic Kerala cuisine experience for the people of Weymouth.

KERALAN CUISINE

The cuisine that inspires White Peppers

Tell them Purdey sent you...

Menu originates from Kerala which is located in the beautiful southwestern coastal region of India. Surrounded by the sea, Kerala is the home to numerous vegetarian and non-vegetarian lip-smacking dishes. Peppercorns, Turmeric, Ginger, Chillies, Curry leaves, Coconut, Mustard seeds and cinnamon are some of the most frequently used spices in Keralan cuisine.

BRIEF HISTORY OF KERALA

Kerala is a state in south India. The name Kerala translates to "The Land of Coconut", Kera meaning coconut in the native language. It's also known as the Land of Spices because of the abundance of spices and medicinal plants that are grown there including Peppercorn. One can trace the origins of the trade of peppercorns back to the region of Kerala, from where it journeyed across the Arabian sea from the Malabar coast to the Early Roman Empire on 120 ships annually, for many people at that time, Peppercorns were too expensive and seen as a delicacy due to its scarcity. This problem was solved in the 15th Century when The King John II of Portuguese sent a reputed sailor named Vasco Da Gama on a mission to find a sea route to India. Thus, Gama became the first European to discover the first sea route to the North Coast of Kerala, which opened the rest of the world to exotic spices including

Tell them Purdey sent you…

peppercorns and cinnamon.

Monday	17:00 – 22:30
Tuesday - Friday	11:30 – 22:30
Saturday	07:30 – 22:30
Sunday	07:30 – 22:30

CAFFEINE   07488 883818

www.caffeineweymouth.co.uk
www.facebook.com/CaffeineWeymouth/
Hello@caffeineweymouth.co.uk

Caffeine is a brand-new venue for the Weymouth. Offering quality coffee and artisan food and pastries in the day and transforming into a vibrant cocktail and craft beer lounge in the evenings.

Nestled on Weymouth's iconic seafront, Caffeine is perfect for coffee enthusiasts and cocktail lovers alike. Proudly brewing the best coffee in Weymouth, our daytime offerings are a delightful blend of fantastic drinks and homemade food. As the sun dips below the horizon, we transition into a vibrant seafront cocktail bar, showcasing the craftiest cocktails Weymouth has to offer. At Caffeine, it's more than just a drink; it's an experience where beachside serenity meets urban flair.

Sunday	09:00 - 16:00
Monday	09:00 - 22:00
Tuesday	09:00 - 22:00

Tell them Purdey sent you…

Wednesday   09:00 - 22:00
Thursday   09:00 - 22:00
Friday   09:00 - 00:00
Saturday   09:00 - 00:00

THE FISH PLACE   07450 924502

www.facebook.com/pages/The-Fish-Place/666015640424685

Used to be Harlequin Grill for 30 years. Family business which becae the fish and chip shop 7 years ago.

Monday - Sunday   08:00 - 22:00

WAFFLICIOUS   07886 860570

www.wafflicious.co.uk/
eat@wafflicious.co.uk
www.facebook.com/WafficiousWeymouth

Wafflicious is situated opposite the glorious Weymouth Beach at 46 The Esplanade, Weymouth. Our team all adore the views from the parlour, and you should come and see them too.

We share some of our favourite moments in Weymouth over on our Facebook page so if you can't quite be here all the time, you can experience life by the seaside through the screen.

Tell them Purdey sent you…

We opened in the beginning of 2022 with the drive to bring smiley faces to our customers and serve you the best desserts. Here at Wafflicious we want to make sure you have the best time and experience at our parlour, and we encourage your feedback.

Our ice cream is produced at Marshfield Farm and to ensure that we are happy with production we went to visit the cows themselves. We are animal-friendly and love seeing your pups enjoying our doggy ice cream.

Monday - Sunday   11:00 - 18:00

BENNYS BEACH HUT
                                      01305 779410

Bubble Tea, Clothes, Gifts, Rock, Ice Cream and Waffles.

ROCKFISH   01305 249040

https://therockfish.co.uk/pages/weymouth-seafood-restaurant
www.facebook.com/RockfishWeymouth

Our Weymouth seafood restaurant is on the Esplanade and enjoys sweeping views overlooking the sandy beach and across the bay. Join us for sustainably caught, fresh, local fish

Tell them Purdey sent you…

landed that day from our boat Rockfisher across the Devon & Dorset coastline, as well as fish selected by us that morning from Brixham Fish Market, which we prepare by the harbour side at dawn to be served to you by lunchtime that day. Your server will talk through the daily selection available, marking each fish species down on your tablecloth and the different ways our chefs cook it to order for you - on the chargrill or crisp fried. We have seating both inside the restaurant and several outside tables to enjoy fresh seafood and enjoy alfresco dining with a canopy and watch the world go by. The Chart Room, our private dining room is also a perfect space for you to celebrate a party or special occasion to enjoy a great meal with friends and family. We have tables outside which are subject to availability and weather.

Monday - Sunday   12:00 - 21:00

BACARO   01305 771113

www.bacaroweymouth.co.uk
www.facebook.com/bacaroweymouth/
hello@bacaroweymouth.co.uk

We are a brand new, local family run, Italian restaurant and bar located on the beautiful Weymouth seafront.

Our passion is carefully thought-out and

Tell them Purdey sent you…

skilfully prepared dishes, to ensure you and yours have a superb meal.

We want to create a venue and atmosphere where you can truly kick-back, relax and enjoy celebrating life's special moments.

We have created a restaurant that will ensure you can have an enjoyable and exciting dining experience; offering the best food service and family friendly ambience possible.

We would love you to join us for Lunch or an Evening meal, so click below to book a table or call us and our team will be happy to answer any questions you may have.

Monday - Sunday   11.00am – 11.00pm

SAMBÔ RODIZIO
BAR & GRILL

01305 457870

https://samborodizio.co.uk/sambo_weymouth/
www.facebook.com/SamboRodizio/
Weymouth@samborodizio.co.uk

We offer unlimited table-side service of 8 cuts of meat for lunch.

More than tradition, Sambô Rodizio is the result of a long walk, from the south of Brazil, with its roots in the countryside of Paraná, where everything started, surrounded by all the tradition and proudness of the Brazilian

Tell them Purdey sent you…

Churrasco served on skewers, the RODIZIO. Originated in the zone of Pampa Southern Brazil, it quickly became a part of Brazil's National Brand.

Sunday	12:00 - 15:00
	17:00 - 22:00
Monday	17:00 - 22:00
Tuesday	CLOSED
Wednesday	17:00 - 22:00
Thursday	17:00 - 22:00
Friday	17:00 - 22:00
Saturday	12:00 - 15:00
	17:00 - 22:00

NOT DOG FRIENDLY

DENBOSSA   01305 766901
hello@denbossa.co.uk

An immersive club in Weymouth seafront. Transport yourself to the party island of Ibiza.

Sunday – Thursday	9am – 10pm+
Friday – Saturday	9am – 5am

KIKA   01305 766901
www.facebook.com/people/KIKAbeach/100063612731896/
hello@kikabeach.co.uk

Vibrant, beach front, tapas bar ready to fulfil

Tell them Purdey sent you…

your socially distanced, booze up needs! Kick back,

Sunday   12:00 - 22:30
Monday - Thursday   12:00 - 23:00
Friday   12:00 - 04:00
Saturday   12:00 - 05:00

THE NOOK   01305 760868

www.facebook.com/thenookcocktailclub/
info@thenookcocktailclub.com
https://thenookcocktailclub.com/

Welcome to The Nook Cocktail Club.

A National award-winning, hustling and bustling independent Cocktail bar and club with cocktails, soul music and dancing at its heart!

Daytimes and early evenings you will find us serving the freshest cocktails to a soundtrack of chilled tunes with beach view seating both inside and outside in our state of the art, covered and heated terrace. Choose from our extensive and forever growing Little Book of Nook Cocktail Menu and impressive back bar… there's literally something for everyone!

When the sun goes down, we really come alive with our resident DJ's leading our very own vinyl revival! Early arrival is recommended as space on the dance floor is strictly first come first serve!

The number one destination for locals and

Tell them Purdey sent you…

visitors alike…come on down to the beach and see what all the fuss is about!

Want Cocktails to Go?

We have recently expanded our 'Cocktail to go' product range which now includes Cocktail Kit Gift Boxes with national delivery options

Monday – Thursday	1700 – 0100
Friday – Saturday	1200 – 0400
Sunday	1700 – 0100
Delivery Hours	
Monday	1600 – 2200
Tuesday – Saturday	1600 – 2200
Sunday	1600 – 2200
Takeout Hours	
Monday -	1600 – 2200
Tuesday – Saturday	1600 – 2200
Sunday -	1600 – 2200

BELLA's CAFÉ   07807 854481

www.facebook.com/bellasweymouth/
bellasweymouth@gmail.com

Open every day for coffee, cake, and delicious homemade lunch on Weymouth Esplanade.

Sunday	CLOSED
Monday	09:00 - 15:30
Tuesday	09:00 - 15:30
Wednesday	09:00 - 15:30

Tell them Purdey sent you…

Thursday	09:00 - 15:30
Friday	09:00 - 16:00
Saturday	09:00 - 16:00

SEACROFT   01305 783140
www.facebook.com/people/Seacroft-Fish-Chips-Weymouth/100063832341246/

CAFÉ BLUE   07789 517513

Cafe Blue on The Esplanade Weymouth enjoys fantastic views, fabulous coffee good choice of food including breakfasts, skinny style and all freshly cooked to order

| Monday, Tuesday, Thursday, Friday, Saturday, Sunday | 09:00 - 15:00 |
| Wednesday | CLOSED |

OLIVETO   01305 839888

Pier Bandstand, The Esplanade   DT4 7RN
https://olivetoweymouth.co.uk/
www.facebook.com/OlivetoWeymouth
hello@olivetoweymouth.co.uk

We are indeed dog friendly for well behaved dogs, we just ask you make a note when booking a table so we can allocate a suitable table.

Monday	CLOSED
Tuesday	17:00 - 20:00
Wednesday	17:00 - 20:00

Tell them Purdey sent you…

Thursday 12:00 - 13:30
17:00 - 20:00
Friday 12:00 - 13:30
17:00 - 20:30
Saturday 12:00 - 13:30
17:00 - 20:30
Sunday 12:00 - 13:30
17:00 - 20:00

PEKING TOWN   01305 768218

www.facebook.com/Pekingtownweymouth/
https://pekingtown.co.uk/

Peking town provides freshly prepared Chinese hot meals served in a friendly open kitchen, situated on the beautiful sea front.

Monday – Thursday 12:00 - 02:00
17:00 - 23:00
Friday 12:00 - 02:00
17:00 - 00:00
Saturday 12:00 - 02:00
17:00 - 00:00
Sunday 12:00 - 02:00
17:00 - 23:00

TOUCIES
BEACH GOODS   01305 785863
62 Esplanade   BEACH SHOP
www.facebook.com/people/Bradburys-News/100063973422034/

Tell them Purdey sent you…

touciesweymouth@gmail.com

THE VIEW (Beach)   01305 839888
www.facebook.com/theviewatweymouth/

A popular cafe situated on Weymouth Esplanade, boasts a spacious decking area for locals and tourist

Monday - Sunday   08:30 - 22:30

THE GOOD LIFE CAFÉ
07576 669111

www.goodlifecafe.co.uk
www.facebook.com/GLC109/
Weymouthgoodlife@hotmail.com

The Good Life Cafe Bistro is family run and is surrounded by miles of sandy beach on the coast of Weymouth, offering exceptional views out to sea and a refreshing seaside atmosphere.

Recently taken over by Carl, Alexandra & family and opening our doors again Tuesday 9th April.

You will find a warm welcome at the Good Life Cafe, Open for breakfast, Lunch & Dinners Tuesday to Saturday And New to the Good Life our Sunday Roast Dinners!

With a brand new menu & a couple of specials the Good Life Cafe Bistro is the perfect place to while away the morning, afternoon or evening with your nearest and dearest.

Tell them Purdey sent you…

Our cakes and desserts are freshly made each day, with an ever changing daily specials menu, to ensure there is always something to tickle your fancy! Our dedication to quality and passion great service is evident in everything from our fine coffee and handmade cakes, to our locally sourced ingredients.

If you just want a quiet place to sit and relax, come and join us for a fresh pot of tea or an indulgent glass of wine or beer, whilst you sit back and admire the beautiful surroundings.

If you're celebrating a special occasion, we would be happy to make sure you have the most memorable day for all the right reasons, simply contact us to discuss your requirements. Carl & Alexandra look forward to welcoming new friends to the cafe. Please feel free to get in touch or just pop in and see us!

Sunday	10:00 - 16:00
Monday - Friday	10:00 - 16:00
Saturday	09:00 - 16:00

WEYMOUTH GIFTS & FANCY DRESS

GIFT SHOP 01305 778090
www.weymouthrockfudgeandgifts.co.uk/
www.facebook.com/Weymouthfancydress/
sales@weymouthfancydress.co.uk
Since 2013

Tell them Purdey sent you…

Weymouth Rock, Fudge & Gifts is the definition of delicious! We are a family ran business founded in 2013, we like to say we are bringing joy to Weymouth, and it's something we hope to be doing for years to come. But we offer more than just high-quality, delicious products. We are a Rock, Fudge and Gift Shop that has become an important part of the local community. We also have a Fancy Dress Branch of the business too.

Come down and meet us and maybe indulge in our famous alcoholic slushies with over 35 alcohols to choose from.

Monday - Sunday   09:00 - 17:00

COASTAL VIBES - The original Weymouth Rock and Fudge Shop
www.facebook.com/people/Coastal-Vibes-The-original-Weymouth-Rock-and-Fudge-Shop/100093617825833/

EDZ
www.facebook.com/Edzweymouth/
Monday – Sunday   10:00 - 16:00

HAPPY DAYS   01305 779255
Monday – Sunday   08:30 - 17:30

Tell them Purdey sent you…

THE WEYMOUTH SHOP

01305 778483

79 Esplanade GIFT SHOP
www.facebook.com/WeymouthShop/

Water sports, Wetsuits, Beach Equipment, Candy, Ice Cream, and so much more on Weymouth Esplanade.

Monday - Sunday   10:00 - 19:30

PREMIER Convenience Store

SANDS AMUSEMENTS

HEDLEY'S

112 Esplanade   ICE CREAM
www.facebook.com/MrWeymouth/

Friendliest gift shop in Weymouth! Open when it's sunny; selling ice cream, beach toys, boats, rock.

CAFÉ NAPOLI

www.facebook.com/people/Cafe-Napoli/61557862773493/

A Weymouth based Italian style cafe, with pizzas from Pizza Napoli

Monday   CLOSED
Tuesday - Friday   10:00 - 17:00

Tell them Purdey sent you…

Saturday   09:00 - 17:00
Sunday   09:00 - 16:00

BLUEBIRD COACHES
Coach Trips

THE GLOUCESTER
01305 777697

www.thegloucesterweymouth.com/
www.facebook.com/thegloucesterweymouthbay/
thegloucester@dndco.uk

The Black Rock Grill is a unique, delicious, healthy interactive dining experience that allows your meal to be presented cooking on the volcanic rocks at your table. All Black Rock Grills are served with chips or jacket potato and a fresh mixed salad.

Our beautiful building is steeped in rich history, having been the summer residence of King George III. After he became very ill in the late 18th century the physicians of the day extolled the virtues of sea air and sea water (for bathing and even drinking!) as a cure for a wide variety of ailments.

His brother, the Duke of Gloucester, owned Gloucester Lodge in Weymouth Bay and offered to lend this to his brother for a seaside holiday. Gloucester House or Lodge was a red brick house built sideways onto the Esplanade

Tell them Purdey sent you...

with a sizeable garden called the Shrubbery. However, it was not big enough to accommodate the entire Royal party comfortably, and the gentlemen were forced to stay in neighbouring buildings.

The King, his Queen and his four oldest daughters arrived in Weymouth at the end of June 1789 to a tremendous welcome. The words "God Save the King" could be seen everywhere – on caps, on windows and even on the waistbands of bathing assistants.

The visit was a resounding success. The Queen announced that King George was "much better and stronger for the sea bathing". Apparently, life in Weymouth exactly suited the King and he returned in 1791 and then almost every year until 1805.

When the King was in Weymouth, the government came to him. Pitt visited him here whilst serving as First Lord of the Treasury and it was in Weymouth in 1798 that the King signed papers elevating Admiral Nelson to the peerage.

Monday - Thursday	11:00 - 23:00
Friday	11:00 - 00:00
Saturday	09:00 - 00:00
Sunday	10:00 - 23:00

Tell them Purdey sent you…

SEA BEATS   01305 767444

www.facebook.com/seabeatsuk/
adam@seabeats.co.uk https://seabeats.co.uk/

Seabeats is a family run Seafood Restaurant its owner and head chef is Adam Foster who was born in Weymouth and studied at Weymouth College.

His first position was at the well renowned Mallams Restaurant on the harbour where Adam continued his learning experience under their Head chef.

He moved from there to The Roundhouse where he held his first Head chef appointment, following that he travelled abroad gaining experience in French and Spanish cuisine.

On his return Adam was appointed the Head Chef at the Crab House Cafe where he held the position for 9 years. In that time they were awarded one Rosette and also awarded Best Seafood Restaurant in England at the English Food Awards.

Adam opened Seabeats in April 2017 and within 18 months were Highly Commended at the Wessex FM Awards and also a finalist in the Dorset Food and Drink awards for Best Seafood in Dorset

Monday	CLOSED
Tuesday - Saturday	17:00 - 22:30
Sunday	CLOSED

Tell them Purdey sent you…

JAYNE'S COFFEE SHOP
07841 909834

LIFESTYLE
Convenience   01305 781153

CROWN ARCADE AMUSEMENTS

ROSSI'S ICES   01305 785557
www.facebook.com/rossisicecreamweymouth/
rossis.weymouth37@gmail.com
www.rossisweymouth.com/

Family run traditional Italian ice cream parlour in Weymouth. Established in 1937 and currently run by the 3rd generation Figliolini.

Winner of 2022 dog friendly business awards - best dog friendly hospitality.

We're Rossi's Ices Weymouth. A traditional Italian ice cream parlour based at the heart of the Weymouth seafront.

Established in 1937 by Fioravanti Figliolini, our ice cream is homemade, with love on the premises following a closely guarded family recipe.

Due to the way that we make our ice cream (in small batches) we can only make a maximum of 2 or 3 flavours per day. However, this does mean that if you are visiting Weymouth for a

Tell them Purdey sent you…

few days, you have the opportunity to try a different flavour every day.

Monday - Sunday   10:00 - 18:00

BOOKS AFLOAT   01305 779774
66 Park Street   BOOKS
www.facebook.com/pages/Books-Afloat/257063451296224

Tuesday – Saturday   10:00 - 17:00
Sunday   CLOSED
Monday   CLOSED

CHUNES   01305 788880
9 Mitchell Street   RECORD SHOP
www.facebook.com/ChunesWeymouth/
chunes2@gmail.com

Chunes is a local independent record store which stocks vinyl and CD's of all genres along with guitar strings, Sheet Music, Accessories, E-cigarettes, and E-Liquid.

Monday   11:00 - 17:30
Tuesday   11:00 - 14:00
Wednesday   11:00 - 17:30
Thursday   11:00 - 17:30
Friday   11:00 - 17:30
Saturday   11:00 - 17:30
Sunday   CLOSED

Tell them Purdey sent you…

THE HARBOUR

The harbour is at the mouth of the River Wey as it enters the English Channel. The original Roman port at Radipole to the north was lost to silting (forming Radipole Lake), and the current harbour further downstream started to develop in the 12th and 13th centuries.

Weymouth Harbour empties into the much larger Portland Harbour to the south and east, which is home to the Weymouth and Portland National Sailing Academy, where the sailing events of the 2012 Olympic Games and Paralympic Games were held.

Weymouth Harbour used to be a port for the cross-channel ferries and is now home to pleasure boats and private yachts.

The Weymouth Harbour Tramway ran along the north side of the harbour to the long disused Weymouth Quay Railway Station. The track was removed during 2020 and 2021 except for two short sections left as a memorial.

Immediately to the north at the harbour entrance is Weymouth Pier, separating the harbour from Weymouth Beach and Weymouth Bay.

Weymouth Pavilion is still standing and hosts a number of shows and events.

Tell them Purdey sent you…

Stone Pier is located on the south side of the harbour entrance.

Immediately to the south near the entrance to the harbour are Nothe Gardens and Nothe Fort on the promontory. Nothe Parade runs along the south side of the harbour front, Wellington Court, the former Red Barracks, built in 1801, is above and overlooks the harbour entrance.

Tell them Purdey sent you…

Tell them Purdey sent you…

THE HARBOUR TERRACE
01305 785012

www.facebook.com/dineontheterrace/

Beautifully situated south facing dining experience on the historic Weymouth harbour. Lunches and private dining specialising in locally caught seafood.

Tell them Purdey sent you…

Monday — CLOSED
Tuesday — CLOSED
Wednesday - Sunday — 12:00 - 15:00

LES ENFANTS TERRIBLES

01305 772270

https://les-enfants-terribles.co.uk/
www.facebook.com/LesEnfantsTerrible/

We are here to make your meal as relaxing and revitalising as possible. Our ethos is to serve locally caught fish and locally made produce to our customers who are usually looking for somewhere where they can relax and unwind with good food and great ambience. Come and be an Enfants Terribles with us.

Established in 2016 by Chef Eric Tavernier, the restaurant took over from Floods as a local seafood restaurant. As Eric who is the owner and Head Chef is French, there is a definite je ne sais quoi to the seasonal menu.

Seafood comes straight from the Harbourside and you will find with Eric's 30 years of culinary experience that the flavours are coaxed to perfection. Eric is always interested in your preferences and is only happy if you are happy so if you have any requests, don't hesitate to voice them.

Here at Les Enfants Terribles we can assure

Tell them Purdey sent you…

you that you will leave satisfied – and be coming back for more !

Monday	CLOSED
Tuesday	12:00 - 14:30
	18:00 - 21:00
Wednesday	12:00 - 14:30
	18:00 - 21:30
Thursday	12:00 - 14:30
	18:00 - 21:30
Friday	12:00 - 15:00
	18:00 - 22:30
Saturday	12:00 - 15:00
	18:00 - 22:30
Sunday	CLOSED

THE LOFT (Unknown as to whether it is open)

VINOLO   01305 789033
https://vinolo.uk/

Our in house wine expert is looking to produce the best wine list available with a great selection of wine by the glass. Our selection of wines by the bottle include wines from Italy, Spain, Portugal, France, as well as Hungary, Georgia and Dorset. Our in house experts make a mean cocktail and our selection of gins currently tops 50.

Our menu is currently changing and we are

Tell them Purdey sent you...

adding more food to drink with a bottle of wine.

Afternoons are for sharing boards and cheese.

We hold regular wine tastings led by our in house wine expert dates are below. We also host gin tastings, fondue and supper clubs.

Private tasting are available both on and off site contact us for more details however minimum numbers are required.

Wine bar, gin bar, Dorset wines.

Monday	CLOSED
Tuesday	CLOSED
Wednesday	17:00 - 22:00
Thursday	11:00 - 21:00
Friday	11:00 - 22:00
Saturday	11:00 - 22:00
Sunday	10:30 - 18:00

TJ's & STEAKASAURUS
Eatery & Bar

01305 778333

www.facebook.com/tjsandsteaksaurus/menu/

We are a family run cafe using local ingredients.

EBIKE CAFÉ @ DEHEERS

01305 786839

www.facebook.com/EbikecafeatDeheers/

Tell them Purdey sent you…

info@ebikecafe.co.uk
https://ebikecafe.co.uk/

The EBIKE CAFE is all about 'Health & Wellbeing'. Drinks, healthy food, service & repairs.

Our philosophy at the EBIKE Cafe is all about 'Health & Wellbeing'. Eating healthy and regular exercise is even more important post the Coronavirus pandemic.

You can join us inside at the EBIKE Cafe or outside in our seating area overlooking Weymouth's picturesque old harbour or you can takeaway, the decision is yours.

We are open for eBike sales. We also service and repair traditional as well as eBike's within the EBIKE Cafe.

Monday – Friday   09:00 - 15:00
Saturday   09:00 - 16:00
Sunday   09:00 - 16:00

CUSTOM HOUSE CAFÉ
01305 771121

www.facebook.com/people/Custom-House-Cafe-Weymouth/100057101483938/

Cafe overlooking Weymouth harbour serving breakfasts, lunches, coffee and homemade cakes and scones.

Monday - Sunday   09:00 - 17:00

Tell them Purdey sent you…

QUAYSIDE   01305 769004

Monday	CLOSED
Tuesday	CLOSED
Wednesday	CLOSED
Thursday - Saturday	10:00 - 14:30
	17:30 - 20:30
Sunday	10:00 - 14:30

THE GEORGE   01305 789635

www.facebook.com/TheGeorgeBarGrill/
feedme@thegeorgebarandgrill.co.uk

Friday	10:00 - 23:00
Saturday	10:00 - 23:00
Sunday – Thursday	10:00 - 22:00

WEYFISH   01305 761277

www.weyfish.com/
www.facebook.com/weyfish/
office@weyfish.com

We're Weymouth's harbourside fishmonger, based in the historic Old Fish Market, with counters full of the freshest Dorset seafood and shellfish, landed daily on the quayside right outside the shop. We're a community business with strong ties to the local fleet, proud of our produce and its provenance, always ready to answer your questions or offer some expert advice.

Monday - Saturday	09:00 - 16:30

Tell them Purdey sent you…

Sunday   CLOSED

HATCH ON THE HARBOUR
                                       07789 136722
www.hatchontheharbour.com
www.facebook.com/hatchontheharbour/
office@hatchontheharbour.com

A deliciously laid back way to enjoy fresh, locally caught, sustainable seafood, straight off the boats. Take a hot grill, a passionate team and a few irresistible favourites. Add a pinch of sea salt and a juicy squeeze of lemon. Place a few tables on the quay, cover, pour in a glass or two and throw in a perfect harbourside view. At Hatch on the Harbour we serve fresh, honest seafood that's all about quality ingredients, taste and flavour. Ready to eat here or take away.

Monday - Saturday   12:00 - 19:00
Sunday   12:00 - 17:00

SHIP INN   01305 773879
www.shipweymouth.co.uk
www.facebook.com/shipinnhw/
shipinn.weymouth@hall-woodhouse.co.uk

Spacious, split-level, quayside pub with bookshelves, storm lamps and a deliciously comforting menu.

Feel at home in this pub on the harbour, with views of the quay – it's the perfect place to eat

Tell them Purdey sent you…

and drink in Dorset

A pub worth talking about

Enjoy hearty pub classics, delicious Sunday Roasts, and our own Dorset-brewed Badger Beers at this picturesque pub on Custom House Quay and watch the boats come and go from the window.

Make the most of every occasion

Join us for lunch after a long walk, a wonderful family dinner, or a much-needed catch-up with friends. Whatever the occasion you'll get a warm and friendly welcome from our team.

And bring the dog!

We're a dog-friendly pub and restaurant, so whether you're popping by for coffee and cake, or staying for dinner you can still spend time with your best friend.

Monday - Thursday	10:00 - 22:00
Friday	10:00 - 23:00
Saturday	10:00 - 23:00
Sunday	11:00 - 22:00

ROYAL OAK   01305 761343

www.facebook.com/TheRoyalOakWeymouth/
https://royaloakweymouth.co.uk/

The Royal Oak is one of Weymouth's oldest pubs situated on the side of the Harbour. Why not come in and enjoy one of many selections

Tell them Purdey sent you...

of alcoholic and non alcoholic drinks !
Friday   12:00 - 00:00
Saturday   11:00 - 00:00
Sunday - Thursday   11:00 - 22:00

THE ANCHOR   01305 761343
https://menyoo.com/the-anchors-weymouth/
Monday - Friday   08:00 - 18:00
Saturday   08:00 - 16:00
Sunday   CLOSED

Tell them Purdey sent you...

THE SAILOR'S RETURN

01305 77337

www.facebook.com/sailorsreturnweymouth/
sailorsreturn@gmail.com

Welcome to the Sailors Return. Situated directly on the harbourside in Weymouth the Sailors Return is one of Dorsets real hidden gems. A traditional and historic pub with a

Tell them Purdey sent you…

warm welcome.
Bed and Breakfast available all year round.
Traditional Cask Ales.

ACROSS THE BRIDGE

Tell them Purdey sent you…

COVE GALLERY
9 Trinity Street   ART GALLERY

VINTAGE WEYMOUTH
25 Trinity Road   COLLECTABLES
www.facebook.com/VintageWeymouth/
Gifts and home décor ideas from past times.

THE BRIDGE FAIR TRADE SHOP

24 Trinity Road
Selling fair trade gifts, cards, toys, and food, with a seating area to enjoy freshly brewed tea or coffee.
thebridgefairtrade@gmail.com

Tell them Purdey sent you…

DRIFT
9 Trinity Street JEWELLERY
www.driftweymouth.com/
Sea inspired gift shop.

BENNETT'S
FISH & CHIPS
14 Trinity Road
https://www.just-eat.co.uk/restaurants-bennetts-fish-and-chips-weymouth/menu

CATCH AT THE OLD FISH MARKET
www.catchattheoldfishmarket.com/
Custom House Quay

TOWN BRIDGE

The Town Bridge is a lifting bascule bridge connecting the formerly separate boroughs of Weymouth and Melcombe Regis. The bridge can be lifted to allow boats access to the inner backwater of Weymouth Harbour, known as Weymouth Marina. The bridge, opened in 1930, is the sixth to have been built across the harbour since 1597 and has been Grade II Listed since 1997. Today, the hydraulically

Tell them Purdey sent you...

operated bridge is raised every two hours, 363 days of the year.

The Bridge was the centre of celebrations on 4 July 2010, the 80th anniversary of its first official opening. The 1930 ceremony was performed by HRH Duke of York who later became King George VI. Cosens-owned paddle steamer, Empress, full of excited school children, was the first vessel to sail under the opened bridge. A procession of highly decorated boats followed, and the harbour was filled with a variety of craft from steam to sail.

The River Wey rises at a spring in Upwey and flows for approximately three miles into Radipole Lake. In Roman times ships were able to sail to the northern shore of Radipole Lake. Remains and evidence have been discovered to verify this. The Wey continues from Radipole Lake to the Backwater, now known as the inner harbour, then through the main harbour into Weymouth Bay.

The river separated the two Parishes of Weymouth (now known as Chapelhay area) and Melcombe Regis (now known as Weymouth). Rivalry flourished between these two ports from early days and continued for many decades, mostly over trading rights at the ports.

In 1570, appointed Commissioners advised a union of the two boroughs and on 1 June 1571, Queen Elizabeth I granted a Charter of Union.

Tell them Purdey sent you...

Although euding still continued for decades. Finally in 1606, a Charter of James I, made the union a working success.

The earliest recorded crossing of the harbour was by the Lelands Ferry in 1533. The boat had been pulled across the harbour by rope – no oars were used.

The first Town Bridge was built of timber in 1597. Wooden piles supported the seventeen-arch bridge with a two-part central drawbridge. The Civil War of 1642-1646 caused structural damage to the bridge. Records reveal many oaks from the New Forest were taken for repair work.

In 1770 another timber bridge was built, extending the quay length by seventy yards. This bridge was a gift by J Tucker, Esq MP, and new warehouses at Weymouth Port allowed for increased trade.

In 1821, plans were produced for a more permanent stone bridge. It was a magnificent structure, built of two graceful arches with a cast iron centre swing section and was completed in 1824. This served the town well for over one hundred years. The swing section allowed larger ships to sail into the backwater. It is recorded that in 1885, it was widened, and the central section altered.

Westham Bridge first spanned the backwaters in 1859, built under the 'Backwater

Tell them Purdey sent you...

Bridge and Road Act 1851'. The wooden structure had a central lifting section, which allowed barges to travel to Westham and Radipole but these were later removed. The bridge opened to the public in 1859 with a toll charge of one halfpenny to cross. It ceased in 1879 when the bridge was registered as a County Bridge.

A backwater dam was built in 1872 to control the water level in Radipole Lake and also to try to stop unpleasant smells at low tide. The now-disused dam can be seen when waters are low. In 1882 the bridge closed for six months for essential repairs. Over £3000 was spent replacing piles and decking.

In 1914, responsibility for the maintenance and preservation of the bridge passed to Weymouth Corporation. Shortly afterwards plans were started to build a new stone bridge. Much land had to be reclaimed at both ends to permit its connection to existing roads. Sluices were built into this bridge to control the water level and these have controlled water levels ever since; the sluices were updated in 2008 and are now electrically controlled.

Large crowds watched the opening of the new Westham Bridge on 13 July 1921 by the then Mayor, Councillor R A Bolt, Chairman of Dorset County Council; Colonel J R P Goodden who unveiled a commemorative

Tell them Purdey sent you…

tablet.

In 1973, a footbridge was designed and added to the side of the bridge. Westham Bridge was closed to through traffic when the new Swannery Bridge was completed in the late 1980s. It has since been used as a car park although it is still possible to cross it on foot and is on the walking route into town.

MARKETS

FARMERS AND MAKERS MARKET
Second Sunday of each Month March - December
New Bond Street,   10am – 3pm

BOWLEAZE POP-UP
First Sunday of each Month April – October
South Lawn, Bowleaze Cove Holiday Park
                             10am – 3pm

FESTIVALS
https://dorsettravelguide.com/dorset-music-festivals/#Chesil_Rocks

SHOWS
Weymouth Pavilion

Tell them Purdey sent you…

https://weymouthpavilion.com/

EVENTS
www.weymouthtowncouncil.gov.uk/events/

SPIRITUALIST WEYMOUTH
The Light Spiritualist Church
www.facebook.com/thelightspiritualistchurch

STONE CIRCLES & FORTS
https://dorset-ancestors.com/?p=2164

HAUNTED WEYMOUTH

NOTHE FORT
https://hauntingnights.co.uk/event/nothe-fort-ghost-hunt-weymouth-dorset/

HAUNTED HARBOUR TOUR
Nothe Fort   September/October
www.weymouthheritagecentre.co.uk/haunted-harbour-tour/

THE PROMENADE

Weymouth's promenade on the seafront is supposedly haunted by an old woman who 'smells of death' and sits on one of the promenade's corner benches. Many have seen

Tell them Purdey sent you…

her.

A man claimed to have seen "The Old Woman of Weymouth" sitting along the seafront one day, in the same spot where his fianceé sat afterwards. His fiancée tragically died of a heart attack the following day.

THE BOOT INN   01305 774851
High West Street, Weymouth,   DT4 8JH
www.bootinnweymouth.co.uk
www.facebook.com/kevsboot/
Monday - Sunday   12:00 - 23:00

Ghosts have been seen at the Boot Inn, a building with a history that dates back to the 14th century.

Extreme temperature dips and furnishings and artwork moved about.

A Victorian sailor and the spirit of a man dressed in a 1930s-style pinstriped suit.

There have been reports of a male choir performing sea shanties at dawn on a regular basis.

MOST HAUNTED: ATHELHAMPTON HOUSE

This great ghost hunting TV show, hosted its first sleepover at Athelhampton with Yvette Fielding and Derek Acorah, this was a spine

Tell them Purdey sent you…

chilling episode.

Its a few years old now, but easily found on streaming services and YouTube

ESCAPE ROOM   01305 773435
escapedungeons@hotmail.com
https://escapedungeons.com/
www.facebook.com/escapedungeons
The Three Chimneys,
143-146 The Esplanade   DT4 7NN
We are a Escape Rooms located on the Seafront of Weymouth, aim of the Game is to Escape within the hour.

TOURS of WEYMOUTH

WEYMOUTH HISTORY TRAIL
We are Weymouth have commissioned some very special ceramic plaques. These tell the stories of 18 of the town's most important locations. Look out for them at the stops along the trail.

WEYMOUTH HERITAGE CENTRE
www.weymouthheritagecentre.co.uk/
weymouthheritagecentre@gmail.com
www.facebook.com/Weymouthtimewalkheritagecentre   01305 858411

Tell them Purdey sent you…

Walking: Haunted Harbour; Plague, Plot and Pestilence; Smuggling; Timewalk

Pirates, Smugglers and Privateers

Boat: 80th Anniversary of D-Day, Story of Portland Harbour, Tall Ships.

Minibus: Moonfleet Smugglers, Defence of Weymouth.

Monday – Friday	09:00 - 17:00
Saturday	CLOSED
Sunday	CLOSED

WEYMOUTH MUSEUMS

TUDOR HOUSE

The Tudor House Museum, often simply known as Tudor House, is an early 17th-century building located close to Brewers Quay and Weymouth Harbour. It remains one of the UK's best-preserved Tudor buildings.

History: Originally, Tudor House was possibly a merchant's property (or possibly a brewery) that fronted an inlet from the main harbour, allowing ships to be moored alongside. However, in the late 18th century, the inlet was filled in, and the building became two small houses under the ownership of Martha Stewart. By 1930 it was condemned. During World War II, it suffered bomb damage and eventually fell into disrepair.

In the 1950s, a local architect, Earnest Warmsley Lewis, acquired the property and restored it to a single dwelling. He furnished it in the style of an early seventeenth-century home of a middle-class family. Thanks to the architect's will, the house became the property of the Weymouth Civic Society, ensuring its future as a showcase of Weymouth's past.

Insight into the Past: A tour of Tudor House provides a fascinating glimpse into life during the heyday of Weymouth as a port for trade and exploration. Guides describe various aspects of daily life, including furniture, clothing, cooking, serving of food, lighting, and candle making.

Educational Opportunities: The tour can be adapted to topics in Key Stage 2 of the National Curriculum, making it a valuable resource for studying Tudor and Stuart times.

Location and Contact Information:
Tudor House, 3 Trinity Street, Weymouth, Dorset, DT4 8TW
01305 779711
Friday and Sunday   10:30 - 4:00
April to October
info@nothefort.org.uk

Tell them Purdey sent you…

9 HISTORY & LOCAL INTEREST

Weymouth originated as two small settlements on either side of the river Wey. These eventually developed into the two separate medieval seaports of Weymouth and Melcombe Regis. There is a possibility that even earlier there might have been a Roman port here, but the evidence is not clear enough to confirm this.

In the Middle Ages wool was exported via Melcombe Regis and wine imported through Weymouth. Melcombe Regis is thought to be one of the ports through which the Black Death entered the country in 1348. The harbour, which they shared uneasily, was at the centre of the economic life of both towns, and from earliest times they argued over it. These quarrels became so bitter that in 1571 Elizabeth I amalgamated them into one borough by Act of Parliament. The Civil War of 1642-1649 caused considerable damage to the town, from which it took a long time to recover.

In the Georgian period, when medical science of the day declared sea bathing to be good for the health, Weymouth began its rise as a seaside resort. George III's decision to come to Weymouth in 1789 for his health, led the town to become the most celebrated and visited watering-place in the land. During the Victorian period the town continued as a popular resort and the harbour flourished with the growth of sea-borne trade with the Channel Islands. The arrival of the railway in 1857 enabled both these aspects of the town's life to continue to grow.

The 20th century with population growth and two world wars had a great impact on the town. The town was badly bombed during World War II and was a key embarkation point for American troops on their way to Normandy in 1944. In the latter half of the 20th century Weymouth's popularity as a seaside resort declined with the rise of cheap foreign holidays and by the end of the century harbour trade had virtually disappeared. The end of cross Channel

Tell them Purdey sent you…

shipping followed not long after..

WEYMOUTH LAND TRAIN
https://weymouthlandtrain.com/
https://www.facebook.com/weylandtrains
The train runs daily – every half an hour from 10am*, taking passengers on a 30min journey of sightseeing and fun.
Board the train on the esplanade opposite M&S Foodhall.
What 3 Words location
coast.gather.deed

Tell them Purdey sent you…

RAF ASSOCIATION

Royal Air Force Association Wings Club
40 Maiden Street Weymouth

Registration Number 231648
Telephone Number 01305 785581

Facebook Page
RAFAWingsClubWeymouth

RAFAWingsClubWeymouth@outlook.com

ABOUT THE AUTHOR

Angela Timms writes novels as MARTINE MOON

Author of:

THE PHOENIX RISING INFINITOLOGY EION SERIES

Many years ago a group of people appeared in the Galaxies. They seemed to be the answer to many problems. They were hard working and very soon integrated into society, gaining positions of power and intermarrying on many of the more prosperous planets.

When they arrived they were known as the "Fallowers" and they had very strong green credentials and benefitted many of the planets they were living on.

Later they changed their name to The Followers and everything began to change. They were in power and they used that power. They pillaged planets for their raw materials and began to convert those who would not follow willingly using drugs and other resources at their disposal.

It was at this time that Mission Command "appeared" to fight against them.

The novels follow the story of Kyla and

Tell them Purdey sent you…

the mysterious Baron Joniel.
    To say any more would spoil the story…

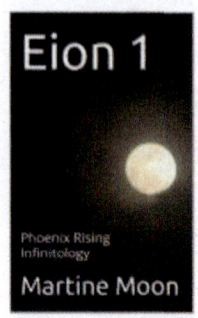

https://www.amazon.co.uk/dp/B0CRJGGLYG

https://www.amazon.co.uk/dp/B0CRPQZW94

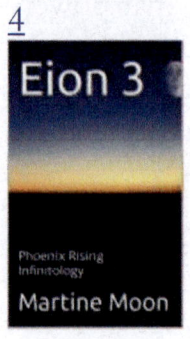

Tell them Purdey sent you…

https://www.amazon.co.uk/dp/B0CRRZK4Z8

https://www.amazon.co.uk/dp/B0CSGC8B34

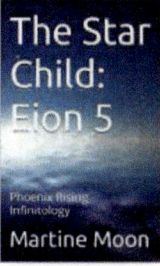

https://www.amazon.co.uk/dp/B0CVNRCLXF

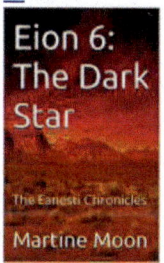

https://www.amazon.co.uk/dp/B0CVNRCLXF

Tell them Purdey sent you…

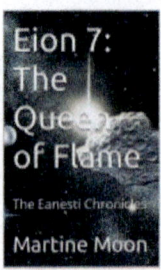

https://www.amazon.co.uk/dp/B0CWZNBCS9

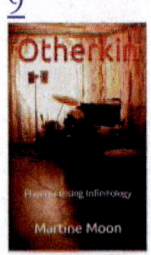

https://www.amazon.co.uk/dp/B0CYDG149L

https://www.amazon.co.uk/dp/B0D23SRQVC

Nemesis is an AI. He was commissioned to help to find a solution to the world's problems. He did that alright, he shut down all computers so that the world could "reboot" while choosing some people to survive in Safe Farms.

Tell them Purdey sent you…

https://www.amazon.co.uk/dp/B0D23SRQVC

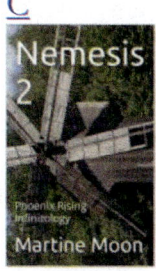

https://www.amazon.co.uk/dp/B0CTTSXPB8

The Books are available on Amazon and both of the series are ongoing.

https://www.facebook.com/PhoenixSpaceOpera

Printed in Great Britain
by Amazon